Intensive Listening Training 2

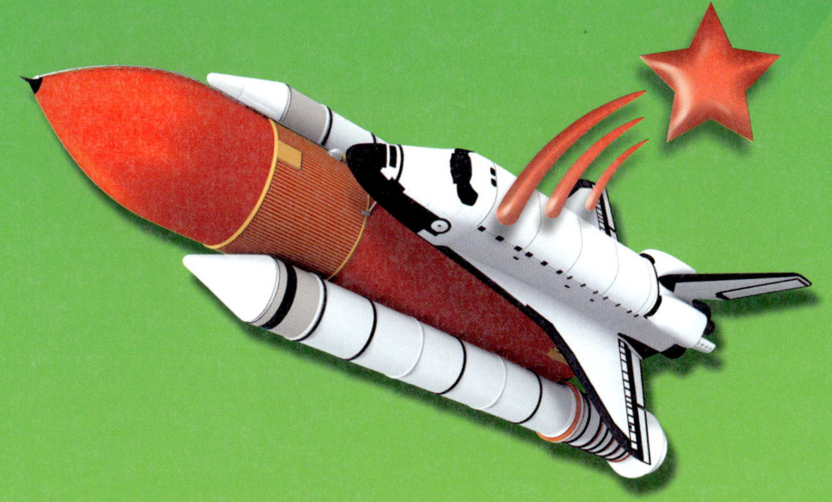

David Bohlke • Anne Taylor

Intensive Listening Training 2

David Bohlke • Anne Taylor

7212 Canary Lane,
Sachse, TX, USA

Acquisitions Editor: Rose Morgan
Content Editor: Liana Robinson
Copy Editor: Tracey Blash
Cover/Design: Highline Studio

http://www.seed-learning.com

ISBN: 978-1-9464-5272-6

10 9 8 7 6 5 4 3 2
22 21 20 19 18

Photo Credits

Contents

How to Use This Book

Intensive Listening Training is a three-book series designed to develop the aural comprehension skills of English language learners at the high-beginning to intermediate level. Units within the series focus on typical speech routines thematically categorized into situational topics. Listening tasks in each unit range from testing discrete listening items to checking general comprehension of short dialogs and talks to completing dictation pages. Each level in the *Intensive Listening Training* series includes more than 180 minutes of audio input for learners to use for practice as they hone their English aural skills.

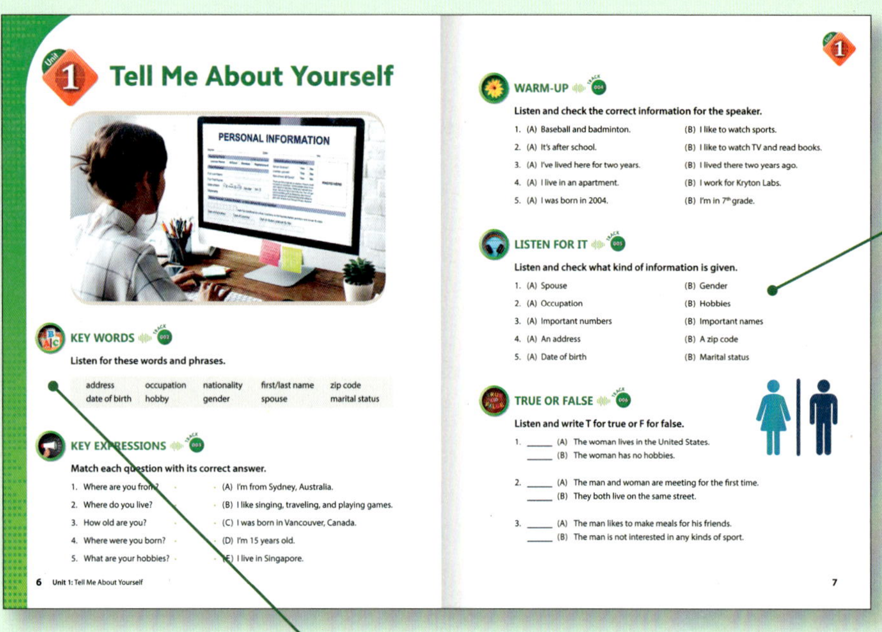

Unit 1 Tell Me About Yourself

KEY WORDS TRACK 002

Listen for these words and phrases.

address occupation nationality first/last name zip code
date of birth hobby gender spouse marital status

KEY EXPRESSIONS TRACK 003

Match each question with its correct answer.

1. Where are you from? · · (A) I'm from Sydney, Australia.
2. Where do you live? · · (B) I like singing, traveling, and playing games.
3. How old are you? · · (C) I was born in Vancouver, Canada.
4. Where were you born? · · (D) I'm 15 years old.
5. What are your hobbies? · · (E) I live in Singapore.

6 Unit 1: Tell Me About Yourself

Unit 1

WARM-UP TRACK 004

Listen and check the correct information for the speaker.

1. (A) Baseball and badminton. (B) I like to watch sports.
2. (A) It's after school. (B) I like to watch TV and read books.
3. (A) I've lived here for two years. (B) I lived there two years ago.
4. (A) I live in an apartment. (B) I work for Kryton Labs.
5. (A) I was born in 2004. (B) I'm in 7th grade.

LISTEN FOR IT TRACK 005

Listen and check what kind of information is given.

1. (A) Spouse (B) Gender
2. (A) Occupation (B) Hobbies
3. (A) Important numbers (B) Important names
4. (A) An address (B) A zip code
5. (A) Date of birth (B) Marital status

TRUE OR FALSE TRACK 006

Listen and write T for true or F for false.

1. ______ (A) The woman lives in the United States.
   ______ (B) The woman has no hobbies.
2. ______ (A) The man and woman are meeting for the first time.
   ______ (B) They both live on the same street.
3. ______ (A) The man likes to make meals for his friends.
   ______ (B) The man is not interested in any kinds of sport.

7

WARM-UP, LISTEN FOR IT, & TRUE OR FALSE

These three activities provide listening practice, progressing from discreet listening at the sentence level in **WARM-UP** and **LISTEN FOR IT** to general comprehension in the short talks in **TRUE OR FALSE**.

KEY WORDS & KEY EXPRESSIONS

The first page in each themed unit introduces useful vocabulary and expressions which the students will hear in the various activities throughout the unit. In **KEY EXPRESSIONS**, students match a question with the best response.

For additional practice, have students check their answers in pairs by role-playing the question-answer dialogs before listening for the answers.

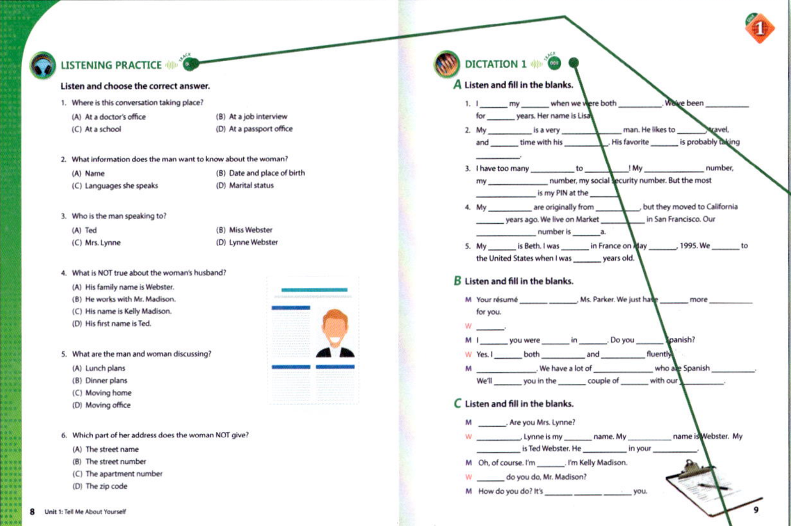

LISTENING PRACTICE

Listen and choose the correct answer.

1. Where is this conversation taking place?
   (A) At a doctor's office (B) At a job interview
   (C) At a school (D) At a passport office
2. What information does the man want to know about the woman?
   (A) Name (B) Date and place of birth
   (C) Languages she speaks (D) Marital status
3. Who is the man speaking to?
   (A) Ted (B) Miss Webster
   (C) Mrs. Lynne (D) Lynne Webster
4. What is NOT true about the woman's husband?
   (A) His family name is Webster.
   (B) He works with Mr. Madison.
   (C) His name is Kelly Madison.
   (D) His first name is Ted.
5. What are the man and woman discussing?
   (A) Lunch plans
   (B) Dinner plans
   (C) Moving home
   (D) Moving office
6. Which part of her address does the woman NOT give?
   (A) The street name
   (B) The street number
   (C) The apartment number
   (D) The zip code

8 Unit 1: Tell Me About Yourself

DICTATION 1

A Listen and fill in the blanks.

1. I ______ my ______ when we were both ______. We've been ______ for ______ years. Her name is Lisa.
2. My ______ is a very ______ man. He likes to ______, travel, and ______ time with his ______. His favorite ______ is probably taking ______.
3. I have too many ______ to ______! My ______ number, my ______ number, my social security number. But the most ______ is my PIN at the ______.
4. My ______ are originally from ______, but they moved to California ______ years ago. We live on Market ______ in San Francisco. Our ______ number is ______ a.
5. My ______ is Beth. I was ______ in France on May ______, 1995. We ______ to the United States when I was ______ years old.

B Listen and fill in the blanks.

M Your résumé ______ ______, Ms. Parker. We just have ______ more ______ for you.
W ______.
M I ______ you were ______ in ______. Do you ______ Spanish?
W Yes. I ______ both ______ and ______ fluently.
M ______. We have a lot of ______ who are Spanish ______. We'll ______ you in the ______ couple of ______ with our ______.

C Listen and fill in the blanks.

M ______. Are you Mrs. Lynne?
W ______, Lynne is my ______ name. My ______ name is Webster. My ______ is Ted Webster. He ______ in your ______.
M Oh, of course. I'm ______. I'm Kelly Madison.
W ______ do you do, Mr. Madison?
M How do you do? It's ______ ______ ______ you.

9

LISTENING PRACTICE

In **LISTENING PRACTICE**, students will answer comprehension questions about a variety of dialogs and short talks.

For additional practice, students can read the transcripts and highlight the key words and expressions from the first page of the unit.

DICTATION 1

In **DICTATION 1**, students revisit some of the dialogs and talks from the previous sections and practice listening for discrete items. Students will listen for individual words and check their ability to recognize sounds and spell them correctly.

Students can compare their answers with a partner, then check the answers as a class. Students working alone should check the transcripts at the back of the book.

LISTENING TEST

The dialogs and talks in **LISTENING TEST** build on the language introduced in the previous activities.

For additional practice, have students work in pairs to create their own dialogs based on the transcripts.

DICTATION 2

As in **DICTATION 1**, students will listen for individual words and check their ability to recognize sounds and spell them correctly.

For additional practice, students can work in pairs and read the transcript together. This will allow students to practice their reading and pronunciation skills in addition to listening and writing.

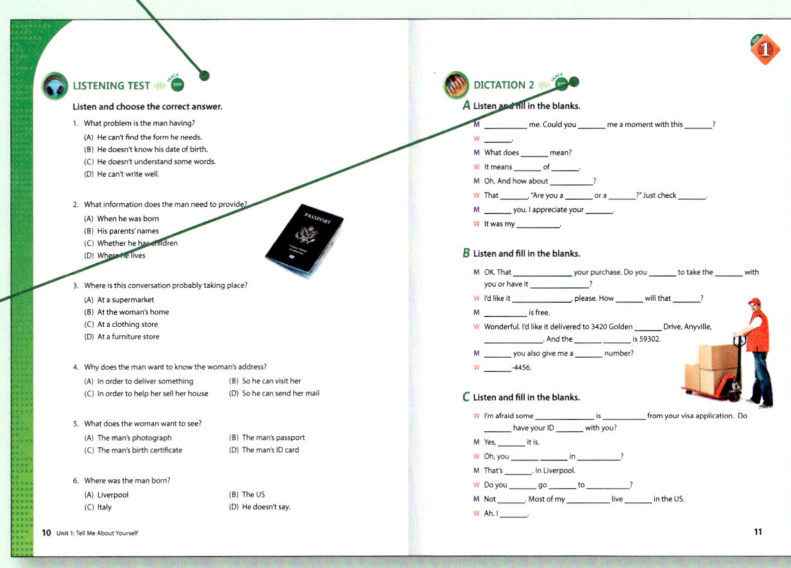

LISTENING TEST

Listen and choose the correct answer.

1. What problem is the man having?
   (A) He can't find the form he needs.
   (B) He doesn't know his date of birth.
   (C) He doesn't understand some words.
   (D) He can't write well.
2. What information does the man need to provide?
   (A) When he was born
   (B) His parents' names
   (C) Whether he has children
   (D) Where he lives
3. Where is this conversation probably taking place?
   (A) At a supermarket
   (B) At the woman's home
   (C) At a clothing store
   (D) At a furniture store
4. Why does the man want to know the woman's address?
   (A) In order to deliver something (B) So he can visit her
   (C) In order to help her sell her house (D) So he can send her mail
5. What does the woman want to see?
   (A) The man's photograph (B) The man's passport
   (C) The man's birth certificate (D) The man's ID card
6. Where was the man born?
   (A) Liverpool (B) The US
   (C) Italy (D) He doesn't say.

10 Unit 1: Tell Me About Yourself

DICTATION 2

A Listen and fill in the blanks.

M ______ me. Could you ______ me a moment with this ______?
W ______.
M What does ______ mean?
W It means ______ of ______.
M Oh. And how about ______?
W That ______, "Are you a ______ or a ______?" Just check ______.
M ______ you. I appreciate your ______.
W It was my ______.

B Listen and fill in the blanks.

M OK. That ______ your purchase. Do you ______ to take the ______ with you or have it ______?
W I'd like it ______, please. How ______ will that ______?
M ______ is free.
W Wonderful. I'd like it delivered to 3420 Golden ______ Drive, Anyville, ______. And the ______ ______ is 59302.
M ______ you also give me a ______ number?
W ______-4456.

C Listen and fill in the blanks.

W I'm afraid some ______ is ______ from your visa application. Do ______ have your ID ______ with you?
M Yes, ______ it is.
W Oh, you ______ ______ in ______?
M That's ______. In Liverpool.
W Do you ______ go ______ to ______?
M Not ______. Most of my ______ live ______ in the US.
W Ah. I ______.

11

Tell Me About Yourself

KEY WORDS

Listen for these words and phrases.

address	occupation	nationality	first/last name	zip code
date of birth	hobby	gender	spouse	marital status

KEY EXPRESSIONS

Match each question with its correct answer.

1. Where are you from? •
2. Where do you live? •
3. How old are you? •
4. Where were you born? •
5. What are your hobbies? •

• (A) I'm from Sydney, Australia.
• (B) I like singing, traveling, and playing games.
• (C) I was born in Vancouver, Canada.
• (D) I'm 15 years old.
• (E) I live in Singapore.

WARM-UP

TRACK 004

Listen and check the correct information for the speaker.

1. (A) Baseball and badminton. (B) I like to watch sports.
2. (A) It's after school. (B) I like to watch TV and read books.
3. (A) I've lived here for two years. (B) I lived there two years ago.
4. (A) I live in an apartment. (B) I work for Kryton Labs.
5. (A) I was born in 2004. (B) I'm in 7th grade.

LISTEN FOR IT

Listen and check what kind of information is given.

1. (A) Spouse (B) Gender
2. (A) Occupation (B) Hobbies
3. (A) Important numbers (B) Important names
4. (A) An address (B) A zip code
5. (A) Date of birth (B) Marital status

TRUE OR FALSE

Listen and write T for true or F for false.

1. _______ (A) The woman lives in the United States.
   _______ (B) The woman has no hobbies.

2. _______ (A) The man and woman are meeting for the first time.
   _______ (B) They both live on the same street.

3. _______ (A) The man likes to make meals for his friends.
   _______ (B) The man is not interested in any kinds of sport.

LISTENING PRACTICE

Listen and choose the correct answer.

1. Where is this conversation taking place?
   (A) At a doctor's office
   (B) At a job interview
   (C) At a school
   (D) At a passport office

2. What information does the man want to know about the woman?
   (A) Name
   (B) Date and place of birth
   (C) Languages she speaks
   (D) Marital status

3. Who is the man speaking to?
   (A) Ted
   (B) Miss Webster
   (C) Mrs. Lynne
   (D) Lynne Webster

4. What is NOT true about the woman's husband?
   (A) His family name is Webster.
   (B) He works with Mr. Madison.
   (C) His name is Kelly Madison.
   (D) His first name is Ted.

5. What are the man and woman discussing?
   (A) Lunch plans
   (B) Dinner plans
   (C) Moving home
   (D) Moving office

6. Which part of her address does the woman NOT give?
   (A) The street name
   (B) The street number
   (C) The apartment number
   (D) The zip code

A Listen and fill in the blanks.

1. I ______ my ______ when we were both __________. We've been __________ for ______ years. Her name is Lisa.
2. My __________ is a very ______________ man. He likes to ______, travel, and ______ time with his __________. His favorite ______ is probably taking __________.
3. I have too many __________ to __________! My ______________ number, my ______________ number, my social security number. But the most ______________ is my PIN at the ______.
4. My __________ are originally from __________, but they moved to California ______ years ago. We live on Market __________ in San Francisco. Our ______________ number is ______a.
5. My ______ is Beth. I was ______ in France on May ______, 1995. We ______ to the United States when I was ______ years old.

B Listen and fill in the blanks.

M Your résumé ______ ______, Ms. Parker. We just have ______ more __________ for you.

W ______.

M I ______ you were ______ in ______. Do you ______ Spanish?

W Yes. I ______ both __________ and __________ fluently.

M ______________. We have a lot of ______________ who are Spanish __________. We'll ______ you in the ______ couple of ______ with our __________.

C Listen and fill in the blanks.

M ______. Are you Mrs. Lynne?

W __________, Lynne is my ______ name. My __________ name is Webster. My __________ is Ted Webster. He __________ in your __________.

M Oh, of course. I'm ______. I'm Kelly Madison.

W ______ do you do, Mr. Madison?

M How do you do? It's ______ ______ ______ you.

Listen and choose the correct answer.

1. What problem is the man having?
   (A) He can't find the form he needs.
   (B) He doesn't know his date of birth.
   (C) He doesn't understand some words.
   (D) He can't write well.

2. What information does the man need to provide?
   (A) When he was born
   (B) His parents' names
   (C) Whether he has children
   (D) Where he lives

3. Where is this conversation probably taking place?
   (A) At a supermarket
   (B) At the woman's home
   (C) At a clothing store
   (D) At a furniture store

4. Why does the man want to know the woman's address?
   (A) In order to deliver something
   (B) So he can visit her
   (C) In order to help her sell her house
   (D) So he can send her mail

5. What does the woman want to see?
   (A) The man's photograph
   (B) The man's passport
   (C) The man's birth certificate
   (D) The man's ID card

6. Where was the man born?
   (A) Liverpool
   (B) The US
   (C) Italy
   (D) He doesn't say.

DICTATION 2

A Listen and fill in the blanks.

M ____________ me. Could you ________ me a moment with this ________?

W ________.

M What does ________ mean?

W It means ________ of ________.

M Oh. And how about ____________?

W That ________, "Are you a ________ or a ________?" Just check ________.

M ________ you. I appreciate your ________.

W It was my ____________.

B Listen and fill in the blanks.

M OK. That ________________ your purchase. Do you ________ to take the ________ with you or have it ________________?

W I'd like it ________________, please. How ________ will that ________?

M ____________ is free.

W Wonderful. I'd like it delivered to 3420 Golden ________ Drive, Anyville, ________________. And the ________ ________ is 59302.

M ________ you also give me a ________ number?

W ________-4456.

C Listen and fill in the blanks.

W I'm afraid some ________________ is ____________ from your visa application. Do ________ have your ID ________ with you?

M Yes, ________ it is.

W Oh, you ________ ________ in ____________?

M That's ________. In Liverpool.

W Do you ________ go ________ to ____________?

M Not ________. Most of my ____________ live ________ in the US.

W Ah. I ________.

Occupations

KEY WORDS

Listen for these words and phrases.

retired	unemployed	flight attendant	nurse	teacher
accountant	waiter/waitress	graphic designer	mechanic	bank teller

KEY EXPRESSIONS

Listen and match each question with its correct answer.

1. What do you do for a living?
2. Is the job still available?
3. How are you enjoying your new job?
4. What do you like about your job?
5. What do you do in a typical day?

(A) Yes. Do you have any experience as a cashier?
(B) I'm a nurse in the health center.
(C) Well, first, I meet the pilot and the other flight attendants.
(D) It's going well so far.
(E) Well, I like my co-workers.

WARM-UP

TRACK 013

Listen and check the correct job for the speaker.

1. (A) Nurse (B) Accountant
2. (A) Flight attendant (B) Pilot
3. (A) Teacher (B) Graphic designer
4. (A) Bank teller (B) Mechanic
5. (A) Retired (B) Unemployed

LISTEN FOR IT

Listen and check the speaker's occupation.

1. (A) Flight attendant (B) Bank teller
2. (A) Retired (B) Nurse
3. (A) Bank teller (B) Bus driver
4. (A) Waiter (B) Graphic designer
5. (A) Teacher (B) Police officer

TRUE OR FALSE

Listen and write T for true or F for false.

1. _______ (A) The woman works at a university.
   _______ (B) The man studies part-time.

2. _______ (A) The man is responding to a newspaper advertisement.
   _______ (B) There is a position as a part-time cashier.

3. _______ (A) The man recently quit his job.
   _______ (B) He doesn't want to be a waiter anymore.

LISTENING PRACTICE

TRACK 016

Listen and choose the correct answer.

1. Who wants the speaker to be a doctor?
   (A) His mother
   (B) His father
   (C) His teacher
   (D) No one

2. What will the speaker definitely do after graduation?
   (A) Become a photographer
   (B) Become a journalist
   (C) Continue studying
   (D) Travel

3. Why does she say she quit her job as an architect?
   (A) The hours were long.
   (B) The pay wasn't good.
   (C) It was too stressful.
   (D) The office was too far.

4. What does she do now?
   (A) She's unemployed.
   (B) She's a part-time architect.
   (C) She cleans homes.
   (D) She styles hair.

5. What does the woman like about her job?
   (A) The pay and benefits
   (B) Her co-workers and boss
   (C) Her vacation and office
   (D) The freedom to take time off

6. What is true about the man's job?
   (A) It is a difficult job.
   (B) He has to make a lot of decisions.
   (C) It gives him a lot of freedom.
   (D) He started it recently.

DICTATION 1 (TRACK 017)

A Listen and fill in the blanks.

1. I'm ________, but you ________ to fasten your ________ ________. The ________ will be landing ________.
2. I just need to ________ your ____________ and I'll get your ________.
3. OK, here is $________, $40, $________, $80, $100. Is there ________ ________ I can do for you ________?
4. I have the ________ for you, ________. And who ________ the spaghetti?
5. ________ show me your ________ license. You ________ ________, sir.

B Listen and fill in the blanks.

I'm a ____________ ________ and will graduate in a few ________. I need to ________ what I ________ to do after I ________. My ________ is a ________, and he wants me to be a ________, too. But that would ________ a lot more ________, and I don't think my ________ are ________ enough. My ________ is a ________. She ________ I should do ________ I want to do. I'm ____________ in ________ and photography, so it might be ________ to be a ________ ________. I'll ________ for a few ________, and then I will ________.

C Listen and fill in the blanks.

I did ____________ that many ________ find ________. I was an ____________ for many years. It was a ________ ________. The ________ was high, but the ________ were so ________. So I quit about ________ ________ ago. I ________ to have my own ________ and be my own ________. I ________ for a certificate in ________ ________ and opened a salon in my ________. I have a lot of ____________, and I can stay ________. I ________ it, but people ________ I'm a little ________.

LISTENING TEST

TRACK 018

Listen and choose the correct answer.

1. What does the man do?

   (A) Pilot
   (B) Flight attendant
   (C) Airplane mechanic
   (D) Airport cleaner

2. What is the busiest part of his job?

   (A) Meeting the pilot
   (B) Doing safety checks
   (C) Helping passengers find seats
   (D) Serving food and drinks

3. What does Kenny do now?

   (A) He's a writer
   (B) He's a businessman
   (C) He's a bank teller
   (D) He's unemployed

4. What does Kenny want to do?

   (A) Become a writer
   (B) Get his old job back
   (C) Become a counselor
   (D) Start a business

5. What did the woman use to do for a living?

   (A) Doctor
   (B) Teacher
   (C) Car sales person
   (D) Mechanic

6. What new activity will she start to do?

   (A) Fix cars
   (B) Teach
   (C) Retire
   (D) Study at the community center

A Listen and fill in the blanks.

W _______ are you ___________ your new _______?

M It's _______ _______ so far.

W _______ do you do on a ___________ _______?

M Well, first, I _______ the _______ and the other ___________ _______________. Then, we do safety checks.

W What ___________ after that?

M That's _______ it gets _______ _______! The _______________ _______ to board, and I have to _______ them find their _______. And _______ we start to _______, it's even ___________ while I hand out _______ and ___________.

B Listen and fill in the blanks.

W How's _______, Kenny? Are you ___________ your lunch _______?

M Didn't you hear? I _______ _______ _______.

W Your ___________ job at the _______?

M Yes. I'm _______________ at the ___________.

W I'm _______ to _______ that.

M Not at all. I want to _______ _______ writing. Now I have the _______.

W Are you _______ _______ get a ___________?

M Yes, and ___________ look ___________.

W Well, good _______, Kenny

C Listen and fill in the blanks.

M I _______ that you ___________.

W Yes, after ___________ _______ as a ___________.

M Do you _______ _______ at all?

W Sure, _______________. But now I can _______ on my own _______!

M That's _______. Are you going to _______ _______ any hobbies?

W Actually, I'm _______ _______ start teaching a _______ on _______ ___________ at the community center once a _______.

M _______.

Describing Things

KEY WORDS

Listen for these words and phrases.

sharp	comfortable	dirty	(be) made of	wood
(be) used for	square	round	rectangular	plastic

KEY EXPRESSIONS

Listen and match each question with its correct answer.

1. Can you guess what it is? •
2. What does it look like? •
3. Can you describe your glasses for me? •
4. How was her dress? •
5. What's that rectangular thing over there? •

• (A) Well, they are metal.
• (B) That will be the table top.
• (C) Is it a cookie?
• (D) It is yellow with red spots.
• (E) It was nice.

WARM-UP

TRACK 022

Listen and check the correct object.

1. (A) A pencil (B) A pen
2. (A) Scissors (B) Rulers
3. (A) Glasses (B) Cups
4. (A) A bus (B) A bicycle
5. (A) A ball (B) The sun

LISTEN FOR IT

TRACK 023

Listen and check what the speaker is describing.

1. (A) A sweater (B) A scarf
2. (A) Chopsticks (B) Knife and fork
3. (A) Coins (B) Matches
4. (A) A door (B) A window
5. (A) An armchair (B) An office chair

TRUE OR FALSE

Listen and write T for true or F for false.

1. ______ (A) The man likes Karl's new car.
   ______ (B) The woman might buy a car like Karl's.

2. ______ (A) The man is making a coffee table.
   ______ (B) It will be rectangular.

3. ______ (A) The man does not like the woman's knives.
   ______ (B) The man will go shopping tomorrow.

LISTENING PRACTICE

Listen and choose the correct answer.

1. What did the man do on the weekend?

   (A) Visit a friend's house (B) Paint a picture
   (C) Improve his home (D) Go to work

2. What does he think about the new color of his bedroom?

   (A) It's sad. (B) It makes him sleepy.
   (C) It's relaxing. (D) It's simple.

3. What is the woman's problem?

   (A) She forgot to buy gifts.
   (B) She forgot to wrap gifts.
   (C) She didn't attach labels to gifts.
   (D) She doesn't like her gift.

4. What is true about Julie's gift?

   (A) It's in a rectangular box.
   (B) It's light in weight.
   (C) It's a pair of shoes.
   (D) It is made of wood.

5. What is NOT true about the gift for the woman?

   (A) It is round. (B) It is metal.
   (C) It is expensive. (D) She can eat it.

6. What did the man probably buy for the woman?

   (A) A cake (B) A soccer ball
   (C) A ring (D) A knife

A Listen and fill in the blanks.

1. It's _______, and I _______ it around my _______. I wear a _______ one made of _______ in the _______.
2. These are _______ and thin, and can be _______ of _______, __________, or metal. They are used for __________.
3. We use these _______ metal objects to _______ things, but they don't __________ have a _______ value.
4. It's usually __________ or ______________ and is made of _______. Every _______ has _______ so that the _______ can come in.
5. It's _______ and ______________ to sit on while you _______ TV or read a _______.

B Listen and fill in the blanks.

I _______ a quiet __________. On __________, I was _______ all _______.
I __________ my house and washed all my _______ __________. On Sunday,
I __________ my __________. It _______ to have _______ walls. But brown is a
_______ _______, so I __________ it light _______. Now it _______ so _______ and
_______. Green is a __________ color, so I _______ I will _______ __________ now.

C Listen and fill in the blanks.

W Oh, no. I've __________ all the __________. But I __________ to put __________ on them.

M Well, _______ we can _______ out what ______________ is. _______ about this _______ __________ box?

W Um, I put Julie's __________ in a __________ _______. How _______ is it?

M It's _______ _______ _______ heavy.

W OK, that's __________ _______. Can you _______ a very _______ box? Like something _______ _______ _______?

M This _______ like _______.

W Great, that's a __________ _______ for __________.

M This is _______. Let's keep _______.

LISTENING TEST

TRACK 027

Listen and choose the correct answer.

1. How doesn't the woman describe the wedding?
   (A) Small
   (B) Fine
   (C) Private
   (D) Pretty

2. How does she describe the wedding dress?
   (A) Traditional
   (B) White
   (C) Short
   (D) Beautiful

3. What is the woman looking for?
   (A) Her math book
   (B) Her pencil case
   (C) A water bottle
   (D) Her glasses

4. What color is the woman's missing item?
   (A) Red and silver
   (B) Blue and white
   (C) Brown
   (D) White

5. Why does Larry need a tie?
   (A) He forgot to wear a tie.
   (B) His tie is dirty.
   (C) He lost his tie.
   (D) He wants to give it to a friend.

6. Which best describes the tie that Larry wants?
   (A) Blue
   (B) Purple and gray
   (C) Green
   (D) Yellow and red

DICTATION 2

TRACK 028

A Listen and fill in the blanks.

M ______ was your ________, Jill?

W ______. I ______ to my ________ wedding.

M Oh ______? How ______ it?

W It was ______ and private, but very ________. My sister was so ______.

M ______ was her ______?

W It was ______. It ________ traditional. It was light ________ and ______, but very ________.

B Listen and fill in the blanks.

W I left my ________ in here after my ______ ______. Have you seen them?

M I found ______ ______ last week. And ______ pencil cases and a ______ ________. Can you ________ your ________ for me?

W Well, they are ______. Actually, they are ______ ______, with a ________ ______ along the side. Do you ______ them?

M I have a pair of ______ ______ ________ and a pair of ______ ________ ______, but nothing that ______ like yours.

W Oh, no. ______ ________ will be so ________.

M I'm sorry. I just don't have ______.

C Listen and fill in the blanks.

W Larry ______ me to take a ______ to his ________. He spilled ________ on ________.

M ______ ______ this ______ one? Or this ________ -and-gray one is nice.

W No. He ______ me which ______ he wants, but I can't ______ it.

M What does it ______ ______? I'll ______ you ______.

W It is ________ with ______ ______.

M He ______ that tie? It's so ______.

W I ______, but Larry ______ it. He says it ______ his eyes ______ ______.

Unit 4 Describing People

KEY WORDS TRACK 029

Listen for these words and phrases.

straight	curly	chin	forehead	in one's 20s
mustache	bald	slim	scar	height

KEY EXPRESSIONS  TRACK 030

Listen and match each question with its correct answer.

1. What does she look like?
2. How did you get that scar?
3. Can you tell me what he looked like?
4. Do you want me to introduce you to my cousin Patty?
5. How was your date?

(A) I fell off my bike.

(B) Great. Ben is so cute.

(C) I don't know. I'm not looking for a girlfriend.

(D) He was tall and thin and had light brown hair.

(E) She's about 50, I guess, and quite overweight.

WARM-UP

TRACK 031

Listen and check the words that describe the speaker.

1. (A) Brown hair (B) Blond hair
2. (A) Long hair (B) Short hair
3. (A) Old (B) Young
4. (A) Thin (B) Overweight
5. (A) Mustache (B) Beard

LISTEN FOR IT

TRACK 032

Listen and check the word that matches the speaker.

1. (A) Scar (B) Slim
2. (A) Handsome (B) Bald
3. (A) Beard (B) Mustache
4. (A) Ugly (B) Handsome
5. (A) Curly (B) Straight

TRUE OR FALSE

Listen and write T for true or F for false.

1. ______ (A) Kim Phillips wears glasses.
   ______ (B) Ralph is Kim's boyfriend.

2. ______ (A) The robber was tall and thin.
   ______ (B) The robber was in his early 30s.

3. ______ (A) Mrs. Parker is about 50 years old.
   ______ (B) Her hair is curly and gray.

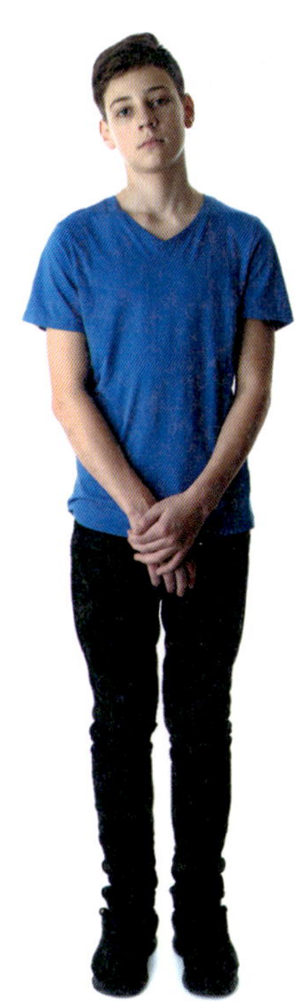

LISTENING PRACTICE

Listen and choose the correct answer.

1. Who is Mr. Madison?
   (A) A teacher
   (B) A student
   (C) A friend
   (D) A comedian

2. What is true about Mr. Madison?
   (A) He made fun of people.
   (B) He was about 13.
   (C) He didn't finish high school.
   (D) He was funny.

3. Why is the announcement being made?
   (A) There is a sale.
   (B) Someone found a boy.
   (C) They're looking for a thief.
   (D) A child is lost.

4. What is NOT true about Sam?
   (A) He is wearing a suit.
   (B) He is young.
   (C) His hair is black and straight.
   (D) He is wearing a cap.

5. What are the two women discussing?
   (A) Their new hairdresser
   (B) Ways to style hair
   (C) What color to dye their hair
   (D) Each other's hair

6. How do the woman feel about their own appearances?
   (A) They are both happy.
   (B) They are both unhappy.
   (C) They have no opinion.
   (D) They do not say.

A Listen and fill in the blanks.

1. I _______ my _______ badly when I was _______, and you can still _______ where the ___________ was.
2. I'm ___________ all my _______, just like my ___________ and grandfather did.
3. The hair on my _______ is starting to _______ very _______ now.
4. My brother Ken is _______________ and wants to be a _______.
5. My hair is full of _______ and ___________. It's _______ to _______ sometimes.

B Listen and fill in the blanks.

Who was my ___________ teacher in _______ ___________? That would be Mr. Madison, my _______ teacher. He was _______—in his _______, I suppose. He _______ math _______, you know. He was _______, always ___________ us laugh. And he had ___________ crazy ______. But he was really ___________ about his ___________ and our ___________. He ___________ us a lot _______ _______ when we needed it.

C Listen and fill in the blanks.

Attention, ___________. We have a _______ _______ in the _______. Please be on the ___________ for a _______, aged _______. His name is _______, and he is ___________ a red ___________ cap and a _______ T-shirt. His hair is _______ and ___________. He was last _______ in the _______ department. If you see this _______, please contact a _______ immediately.

Listen and choose the correct answer.

1. Why does the woman want to introduce her cousin to the man?
   (A) Because he doesn't have a girlfriend
   (B) Because her cousin wants to meet him
   (C) Because her cousin doesn't have any friends
   (D) Because she wants his opinion about her cousin

2. What is NOT true about the woman's cousin?
   (A) She is tall.
   (B) She's pretty.
   (C) She has blue eyes.
   (D) She is short.

3. How did the man get his scar?
   (A) A shark attacked him.
   (B) He was hit by a bike.
   (C) He had an accident.
   (D) The woman hit him.

4. What does the woman think of the cause of the scar?
   (A) It's boring.
   (B) It's exciting.
   (C) It's shocking.
   (D) It's scary.

5. How does Cindy NOT describe Ben's appearance?
   (A) Cute
   (B) Handsome
   (C) Tall
   (D) Brown haired

6. How does she describe his personality?
   (A) Boring
   (B) Uninteresting
   (C) Talented
   (D) Artistic

DICTATION 2

TRACK 037

A Listen and fill in the blanks.

W ______ don't have a ______________, do you, Joe?

M Me? No. Why?

W Do you ______ me to ______________ you to my __________ Patty?

M I don't ______. I'm not __________ for a ______________.

W Well, she is __________. She has ______ ______ hair, blue ______, and she is very ______.

M I don't ______ about that. What is she ______?

W She is very ______. She is ______, too, but kind of serious.

M OK. ______ can I ______ her?

B Listen and fill in the blanks.

W I didn't ______ you had a ______ ______ on your ______.

M This? Oh, ______. I've had it ______ ______.

W ______ did you get that ______?

M I ______ ______ my ______. And I __________ on a ______ stick.

W That's all? I __________ it would be something like a ______ ______. I mean—you ______ a lot.

M Hey, I'm ______ if it's not an __________ story. It really ______, you ______!

C Listen and fill in the blanks.

M ______ was your ______, Cindy?

W ______. Ben is so ______.

M You ______ him then?

W Oh yes. He is ______, __________, and has beautiful ______ ______.

M ______ did you ________ about?

W He's very ______________. He can ______ and ______, too, so he's really __________.

Finding Places

KEY WORDS

TRACK 038

Listen for these words and phrases.

kitty corner to	avenue	across from	behind	in front of
on the corner	block	turn left/right	intersection	traffic light

KEY EXPRESSIONS

Listen and match each question with its correct answer.

1. Can you tell me how to get there? •
2. Do you know the street address? •
3. Is there a supermarket near here? •
4. Can I walk there from here? •
5. Where are you now? •

• (A) I'm at the corner of McGregor and Park.
• (B) Just go straight until you get to Bedford.
• (C) No, it's too far.
• (D) Not in this area.
• (E) She lives at 106 Bedford Road.

Listen and check where the hotel is located.

1. (A) Across from the park — (B) Behind the park
2. (A) Next to the bank — (B) Not next to the bank
3. (A) Behind the post office — (B) In front of the post office
4. (A) Over the supermarket — (B) Kitty corner to the supermarket
5. (A) To the right of the school — (B) To the left of the school

LISTEN FOR IT

Listen and check what the speaker says to do.

1. (A) Turn at the fourth traffic light — (B) Turn at the first traffic light
2. (A) Go east — (B) Go west
3. (A) Walk until the third street — (B) Walk until Third Street
4. (A) Turn left before the library — (B) Turn left after the library
5. (A) Go up Lake Avenue — (B) Go up to Lake Avenue

TRUE OR FALSE

Listen and write T for true or F for false.

1. ______ (A) Shelly lives on Bedford Road.
   ______ (B) The man will take the woman to Shelly's house.

2. ______ (A) The post office is located on 12th Street.
   ______ (B) The woman suggests taking the 33-1 bus.

3. ______ (A) There is a supermarket in the area.
   ______ (B) The store is a five-minute walk.

LISTENING PRACTICE

Listen and choose the correct answer.

1. What is the woman's address?
   (A) 1618 Lincoln Way
   (B) 1680 Lincoln Way
   (C) 6018 Lincoln Way
   (D) 6080 Lincoln Way

2. What should you do at the intersection of Second Avenue and Henderson Street?
   (A) Turn right
   (B) Turn left
   (C) Go straight
   (D) Go north

3. Who is having a party?
   (A) John and Jameson
   (B) Cameron
   (C) Mark and Edward
   (D) Lexington

4. Where is the apartment building?
   (A) On Lexington Avenue, in front of Jameson Foods
   (B) On Lexington Avenue, behind Jameson Foods
   (C) On 8th Street, to the right of Jameson Foods
   (D) On 8th Street, to the left of Jameson foods

5. Which way should the speakers go at the traffic light?
   (A) Left
   (B) Right
   (C) Straight
   (D) Kitty corner

6. Why is the woman confused?
   (A) She can't see the traffic light.
   (B) There are two banks.
   (C) There is no bank.
   (D) She can't find her map.

DICTATION 1

TRACK 044

A Listen and fill in the blanks.

1. Turn ________ at the ________ traffic ________.
2. Go ________ for ________ ____________.
3. ________ until you ________ to the ________ street.
4. ________ a left ________ you ________ the library.
5. Go ________ Lake Avenue ________ you ________ a church.

B Listen and fill in the blanks.

I'll give you ________________ to get to my ________. Listen ________________ or ________ them down. The address is ________ Lincoln Way. Got that? 1680 ___________ Way. Take ___________ Avenue—it's the ___________ route. Go ___________ until you come to the ________________ of Second Avenue and ________________ Street. There, ________ a ________, go ___________ for another ________ blocks, and you'll ________ to Lincoln Way. Turn ________, and look for a ________ ________.

C Listen and fill in the blanks.

John, this is Cameron. Text me ________ you get this ___________. There's a party ___________ at ________ and Edward's ________. Do you ________ where they ________? It's on Lexington ___________. From your ________, go ________ on Lexington until you ________ to Jameson Foods. They live ___________ ________. Park your car at the ________, and ________ for a ________ apartment building with ________ stripes. They live in ______________ ________. Hope to ________ you around ________.

LISTENING TEST

Listen and choose the correct answer.

1. Where is the traffic light?
   (A) On Davis Street
   (B) On Mayfair Lane
   (C) By the sporting goods store
   (D) By the bookstore

2. Where is the sporting goods store?
   (A) Next to the bookstore
   (B) Around the corner from the bookstore
   (C) Above the bookstore
   (D) Below the bookstore

3. Where is the conversation taking place?
   (A) On the 8th block
   (B) On 8th Street
   (C) On 2nd Avenue
   (D) On 2nd Street

4. Where is Second Avenue?
   (A) In front of them
   (B) 8 blocks away
   (C) One block away
   (D) In another city

5. Where is Andrew calling from?
   (A) Mary's apartment
   (B) The street
   (C) The park
   (D) His home

6. What should Andrew do when he sees a men's clothing store?
   (A) Continue straight ahead
   (B) Turn at the crosswalk
   (C) Go west
   (D) Turn the corner

DICTATION 2

A Listen and fill in the blanks.

W ________ me. Is there a ________ around ________?

M ________, there's ________ on ________ ________.

W And ________ is that?

M Oh, ________ up this ________. This is Mayfair ________. ________ it up to the ________ ________.

W Yes . . .

M Take a ________, and go ________ ________. That's Davis.

W ________ . . .

M You'll ________ a ________ sporting goods ________. The bookstore's ________ that.

W ________ ________ very ________.

B Listen and fill in the blanks.

M ________ me, but is this the ________ to the ________ ________?

W No. It's ________ in ________ ________.

M ________ this ________ Avenue?

W ________, this is Second ________.

M Oh ________. ________ is Second ________?

W It's about ________ ________ south of ________.

M I see. ________.

C Listen and fill in the blanks.

W Hello.

M Hey ________! It's Andrew. I can't ________ your ________.

W ________ are you ________?

M I'm at the ________ of McGregor and ________.

W You're ________. Just walk ________ for a few ________. You'll see a ________ clothing ________ on the ________. Keep ________ straight, and ________ the ________. I'm the ________ door on the ________.

M Got it. ________ you ________.

Making Plans

KEY WORDS

Listen for these words and phrases.

definitely	probably	predict	in (an hour / a week)	possible
plan	someday	might	promise	hope

KEY EXPRESSIONS

Listen and match each question with its correct answer.

1. What are you going to do after you graduate?
2. What are you doing this weekend?
3. What are your summer plans?
4. Have you made any New Year's resolutions?
5. What do you think you'll be doing thirty years from now?

(A) I'm meeting my sister on Saturday at the airport.
(B) I have no idea what I want to do with my life.
(C) I'm going to summer school in July.
(D) I'll probably be working in an office.
(E) This year I want to lose weight and learn Spanish.

WARM-UP

Listen and check the correct time expression.

1. (A) In a few minutes (B) In four minutes
2. (A) 6:15 (B) 5:45
3. (A) In June (B) Soon
4. (A) Next year (B) In two years
5. (A) Someday (B) Sunday

LISTEN FOR IT

Listen and check what will probably happen next.

1. (A) Susan will call Angela. (B) Angela will call Susan.
2. (A) The waiter will bring a menu. (B) They will pay for their meal.
3. (A) Bob will buy gas. (B) Bob will pay a bill.
4. (A) They will get off the bus. (B) They will get on the bus.
5. (A) He'll try on the jacket. (B) He'll choose a different jacket.

TRUE OR FALSE

TRACK 051

Listen and write T for true or F for false.

1. ______ (A) Stan's sister is going to visit this weekend.
   ______ (B) Stan will go to a basketball game and the zoo this weekend.

2. ______ (A) The woman will graduate from college soon.
   ______ (B) The woman is sure she wants to be a writer.

3. ______ (A) Alice wants to lose weight.
   ______ (B) Daniel hopes to read more books.

LISTENING PRACTICE

Listen and choose the correct answer.

1. How old is the speaker?
   (A) 20 (B) 21
   (C) 22 (D) 23

2. What is NOT true about the speaker?
   (A) She wants to get married someday.
   (B) She hopes to work with computers.
   (C) She will graduate in two years.
   (D) She is planning to attend graduate school.

3. Why is the woman discussing the doctor's appointments?
   (A) There have been many changes.
   (B) The doctor is forgetful.
   (C) The speaker is leaving early today.
   (D) It's her first day of work.

4. When is the doctor free?
   (A) Between 10 and 12 (B) Between 12 and 12:30
   (C) At 12:30 (D) After 1:30

5. What does the man think he will be doing in the future?
   (A) Working in a park (B) Working on the weekends
   (C) Working in an office (D) Working for the woman

6. What does the man think of the woman's vision of the future?
   (A) Realistic (B) Unrealistic
   (C) Very likely (D) Possible

DICTATION 1

A Listen and fill in the blanks.

1. ________, Susan ________ you to ________ her right ________.
2. ________, may we ________ the ________ menu?
3. Look, Bob. You got a warning ________ from the ________ company. You ________ to ________ the bill ________.
4. ________ your ________ ready. Here ________ the ________.
5. I ________ this ________. Do you ________ it will ________ me?

B Listen and fill in the blanks.

________ ask me ________ I want to ________ in the ________. That's a ________ question to ________. I'll ________ next ________, when I'm ________, so I ________ to make some ________. I ________ go to ________ school ________ year. But I ________ go ________. I ________ that for ________. I want to ________ a job in the ________ ________. I'll ________ get married ________, but I don't ________ when. It's ________ that I will have ________. But I'm not ________. I like ________, but I want to have a ________. I'll ________ that with my ________.

C Listen and fill in the blanks.

________ me, Doctor Lynne? ________ we go over your ________ for ________? As you ________, I will be ________ a little ________ today. You have ________ appointments with ________ this morning, from ________ to ________. At 12:30, Dr. Carrington will be ________ by to ________ some things. You have a ________ at ________, and that should ________ for about ________ an hour. For the ________ of the ________, you can see you will be pretty ________. I'll be ________ until ________ to ________ any ________.

LISTENING TEST

Listen and choose the correct answer.

1. What will Megan NOT do in August?
   (A) Go to summer school
   (B) Go to Dallas
   (C) Get married
   (D) See her parents

2. When will she see her parents?
   (A) The first week of August
   (B) After her friend's wedding
   (C) During summer school
   (D) On August 5th

3. Why can't they get together at 5:00?
   (A) The woman is working.
   (B) The woman has a meeting.
   (C) The woman is having dinner.
   (D) The woman is meeting Greg.

4. What is NOT true about their arrangement?
   (A) It's on Friday.
   (B) It's at 7:30.
   (C) It's at a café.
   (D) Only two people will be there.

5. What is NOT something that the man wants his friends to do?
   (A) Walk
   (B) Ride a bike
   (C) Drive more
   (D) Take a bus

6. What does the man think will happen if we drive less?
   (A) It will harm the Earth.
   (B) The air will be cleaner.
   (C) There will be more public transportation.
   (D) Nothing will change.

DICTATION 2

A Listen and fill in the blanks.

M ________ are your ________ ________, Megan?

W Well, I'm going to ________ ________ in ________ and then going to ________.

M Dallas? ________ are you ________ there?

W My ________ is getting ________ on ________ 5th, so I'll ________ her wedding.

M And ________ that?

W I'll ________ my ________ for a ________ and then return ________.

M That ________ like a ________ ________.

B Listen and fill in the blanks.

M Do you ________ to get ________ on ________?

W What ________?

M I'm ________ Greg at ________. ________ us then.

W I ________. I have to ________ till ________.

M Meet us ________ for ________ then.

W ________. How about ________?

M Sounds ________. ________ to the Vega Café.

W I'll ________ ________.

C Listen and fill in the blanks.

________ I feel very ________ about the ________. ________ do so many ________ that ________ the Earth. My ________ drive ________. I'm trying to ________ them to ________, ride ________, or use ________ transportation. I ________ that if we all ________ using ________ at ________ one day a ________, the ________ will be much ________ polluted. ________ don't you ________?

In the Past

KEY WORDS

Listen for these words and phrases.

last	ago	since	previous	remember
memory	childhood	used to	experience	made

KEY EXPRESSIONS

Listen and match each question with its correct answer.

1. Do you remember Grandma's house? • • (A) I was at Terry's house.
2. Did you see Laura last night? • • (B) I have lots of good memories of her house.
3. Where have you been? • • (C) No, we got together night before last.
4. What is your earliest memory? • • (D) Great.
5. How was your trip? • • (E) Um, maybe when my sister was born.

WARM-UP

TRACK 058

Listen and check the correct time expressions.

1. (A) On the 7th (B) A week ago
2. (A) Last year (B) Two years ago
3. (A) For two years (B) For four years
4. (A) At 7:15 (B) At 7:45
5. (A) In time (B) On time

LISTEN FOR IT

TRACK 059

Listen and check what probably just happened.

1. (A) Someone opened the door. (B) Someone knocked on the door.
2. (A) They finished eating the entrees. (B) They finished eating dessert.
3. (A) The woman cleaned the house. (B) The woman took a shower.
4. (A) The flight arrived. (B) The flight departed.
5. (A) David received a gift. (B) David gave a gift.

TRUE OR FALSE

TRACK 060

Listen and write T for true or F for false.

1. ______ (A) The woman saw Laura two nights ago.
   ______ (B) The woman and Laura had dinner at a great restaurant.

2. ______ (A) The speakers used to go to their grandmother's house.
   ______ (B) One time, they made their grandmother very angry.

3. ______ (A) The woman is speaking to her son.
   ______ (B) The boy forgot to tell his mother where he was.

LISTENING PRACTICE

Listen and choose the correct answer.

1. Who is the woman likely speaking to?
   (A) Her father
   (B) Her boss
   (C) Her teacher
   (D) A possible employer

2. When did the woman start working at Semtex Corporation?
   (A) 2010
   (B) 2012
   (C) 2014
   (D) 2016

3. How many brothers and sisters does the man have?
   (A) A brother and a sister
   (B) A brother and two sisters
   (C) Two brothers and a sister
   (D) Two brothers and sisters

4. What happened when the speaker was 12?
   (A) He moved to the countryside.
   (B) He got another sister.
   (C) His family moved to the city.
   (D) His family sold their apartment.

5. How old was the woman when her sister was born?
   (A) One
   (B) Two
   (C) Three
   (D) Four

6. How did the man feel about school as a child?
   (A) He hated it.
   (B) He loved it.
   (C) He preferred to be home-schooled.
   (D) He had no strong feelings about school.

DICTATION 1

A Listen and fill in the blanks.

1. ________ you ________ that, Roseanne? ________ you ________ the door, ________?
2. I ________ some ________ for a ________ treat. May we ________ see the ________ ________?
3. I ________ so much ________ now.
4. I'm ________ we ________ on time. But we ________ to go through ________ and Immigration ________.
5. ________, it ________ so ________ of you. The ________ fits perfectly.

B Listen and fill in the blanks.

Thank you for ________ me for the ________, sir. I ________ from university in ________ with a ________ in finance. I ________ work the ________ year as a ________ for Wilson Jewelers. I ________ there for ________ years, and then I ________ to graduate ________. I got my master's ________ in business administration in ________. ________ then, I have been ________ as the ________ regional ________ manager at Semtex Corporation. I have a proven ________ of sales, and I have ________ accounts worth ________ $34 million this ________ alone. My ________ experience ________ me ________ for this ________.

C Listen and fill in the blanks.

I had a ________ ________. I am the ________ of ________ children. I have two ________ brothers and a ________. We often ________ together as ________. We ________ to play basketball, ________, and go ________ every summer. It ________ like I was ________ alone. ________ I was ________, we ________ in the ________, but then my ________ got a new ________, so we ________ to a city. Suddenly, we ________ living in an ________ on the ________ floor. ________ of us ________ it very much.

LISTENING TEST

Listen and choose the correct answer.

1. Why didn't George answer the woman's phone call?
   (A) He was at the hospital.
   (B) He lost his phone.
   (C) He was in a meeting.
   (D) His phone was off.

2. What is the man going to do today?
   (A) Visit the hospital
   (B) Call the woman
   (C) Give a report
   (D) Go to work late

3. Where did the woman go?
   (A) On a bus tour
   (B) Austria
   (C) To Sydney's house
   (D) A cruise

4. What kind of accommodation did the woman NOT use?
   (A) Hotels
   (B) Camping
   (C) Private homes
   (D) Small inns

5. Why is the woman surprised?
   (A) She received a beautiful birthday card.
   (B) Her son made a meal for her birthday.
   (C) Her daughter made a birthday cake.
   (D) Her husband made dinner for her.

6. What is NOT something that Billy made?
   (A) Apple juice
   (B) Toast
   (C) Coffee
   (D) Bacon and eggs

DICTATION 2

TRACK 064

A Listen and fill in the blanks.

W Hey, George. I ________ to ________ and text you last ________. ________ didn't you ________?

M Sorry. I was ________ really ________ last night, so I ________ off my ________ and ________ to bed early.

W Are you ________ now?

M I ________, but I ________ have a bit of a ________ and my ________ really hurts.

W I'm ________ to hear that. ________ I get ________ for you?

M No, I'm just ________ to go home ________ after this ________. I have to ________ a sales ____________. Then I'm ________ back to ________.

B Listen and fill in the blanks.

M ____________ home. How ________ your ________?

W Great.

M Where ________ you ________, ________?

W We ________ a ________ tour in ____________.

M That's ________. Did you ________ mostly in Sydney or ________ you ____________ around?

W We ________ all over. Like I ________, it ________ a bus ________.

M How ________ the ________________?

W We usually ____________ in ____________, but sometimes we ________ camping or ____________ in ________ private inns.

C Listen and fill in the blanks.

M Happy ____________, ________.

W Oh, Billy. ________ you. What a ____________!

M Look. I ____________ you ________________, and Susan ____________ up the ____________.

W How ________ of you two!

M I made ________ and eggs, ____________ juice, toast, and ____________.

W It looks ________________. Thanks ________.

Making Comparisons

KEY WORDS

Listen for these words.

better	worse	more	less	least
happier	modern	popular	wetter	easiest

KEY EXPRESSIONS

Listen and match each question with its correct answer.

1. Which city did you like more? •	• (A) I think the red one is a bit better.
2. Which jacket is better quality? •	• (B) Probably the bus.
3. What's the best way to go downtown? •	• (C) I think London was better.
4. Is the bus quicker than the subway? •	• (D) Somewhere cheap, but I don't know yet.
5. Which hotel will you be staying at in Hong Kong? •	• (E) I'd say they both take the same time.

WARM-UP

TRACK 067

Listen and check the correct information.

1. (A) Bill is older. (B) Paul is older.
2. (A) Bill is heavier. (B) Paul is heavier.
3. (A) Bill is richer. (B) Paul is richer.
4. (A) Bill has more children. (B) Paul has more children.
5. (A) Bill is more popular. (B) Paul is more popular.

LISTEN FOR IT

TRACK 068

Listen and check the correct information.

1. (A) Seattle is wetter. (B) London is wetter.
2. (A) Becky sings better. (B) Jill sings better.
3. (A) Ron got a higher grade. (B) Joe got a higher grade.
4. (A) The blue car is cheaper. (B) The white car is cheaper.
5. (A) Mr. Lee works more. (B) Mr. Kim works more.

TRUE OR FALSE

TRACK 069

Listen and write T for true or F for false.

1. _______ (A) Linda preferred *Road Chase II* to *Road Chase I*.
   _______ (B) *Road Chase II* wasn't as long as *Road Chase I*.

2. _______ (A) London had better nightlife than Paris.
   _______ (B) The people in London weren't as friendly as those in Paris.

3. _______ (A) The black jacket is less expensive.
   _______ (B) The red jacket is lighter.

LISTENING PRACTICE

Listen and choose the correct answer.

1. Who is the most athletic child?

   (A) Peter (B) Beth
   (C) Danny (D) It doesn't say.

2. Who is the least musical child?

   (A) Danny (B) Peter
   (C) Beth (D) It doesn't say.

3. Which class is the least difficult for the speaker?

   (A) English (B) Science
   (C) P.E. (D) History

4. Which class is the most boring for the speaker?

   (A) Science (B) P.E.
   (C) Math (D) History

5. What does the woman want to know?

   (A) Where to park downtown
   (B) What transportation to use
   (C) Where to catch the bus
   (D) How much the subway costs

6. Why does the man prefer the bus?

   (A) It's quicker than the subway.
   (B) It's cheaper than the subway.
   (C) It's less crowded than the subway.
   (D) It stops nearer his house than the subway.

DICTATION 1

A Listen and fill in the blanks.

1. It _______ _______ in Seattle _______ in London.
2. Becky _______ much _______ than Jill.
3. On the _______, Ron got a _______, but Joe _______ an _______.
4. The _______ car isn't _______ expensive _______ the _______ one.
5. Mr. Lee _______ 10 hours _______ per week _______ Mr. Kim does.

B Listen and fill in the blanks.

I have _______ wonderful _______. The _______, Beth, will be in _______ next _______. Next is Danny, who is _______, and then _______-_______-old Peter. _______ is the _______ athletic. Peter _______ some sports, but Beth doesn't _______ any _______ at all. She loves _______ and can _______ well and play _______ musical _______. Peter _______ interested in _______, but we'll see. Danny isn't _______ at all. All _______ are _______, and I wouldn't _______ say which one I _______ is the _______.

C Listen and fill in the blanks.

I like _______ a lot. My _______ subject is _______. I find it _______ _______ interesting, but also the _______ _______. I _______ get Bs in that _______. The _______ class by _______ is _______. P.E. is the _______ _______—I love _______ sports. I find math _______ pretty _______, but not _______ _______ boring as _______. That's the _______.

LISTENING TEST

TRACK 072

Listen and choose the correct answer.

1. Which is the most convenient hotel?
   - (A) St. George
   - (B) Park Lane
   - (C) Crown Royal
   - (D) It doesn't say.

2. Which hotel is the least expensive?
   - (A) St. George
   - (B) Park Lane
   - (C) Crown Royal
   - (D) It doesn't say.

3. What is the cheapest way to get from Vienna to Budapest?
   - (A) Air
   - (B) Bus
   - (C) Train
   - (D) Boat

4. Which mode of transportation takes the longest time?
   - (A) Bus
   - (B) Train
   - (C) Boat
   - (D) Air

5. Which apartment is the cheapest?
   - (A) The first one
   - (B) The second one
   - (C) The third one
   - (D) It doesn't say.

6. What is NOT true about the second apartment?
   - (A) It is the least modern.
   - (B) It is smaller than the first one.
   - (C) It is bigger than the third one.
   - (D) It is less expensive than the third one.

DICTATION 2

TRACK 073

A Listen and fill in the blanks.

M Which ________ will you be ____________ at in ________ ________?

W I don't ________ yet.

M The St. George is the ________ ________________, but of ____________ is the most ______________.

W ________ about the ________ ________?

M It's ________, yes, but ________ ________ cheap ________ the Crown Royal if you ________ to save ________.

W Yes, but the Crown Royal is so ________________. It's the ____________ from all the ____________ that I want to ________.

B Listen and fill in the blanks.

W ________ I ________ you?

M Yes, ________ can I get ________ ____________ to Budapest?

W Well, you have ________ choices—________, bus, ________, or air.

M Which is the ____________?

W ________. There are ____________ from $________. The ____________ cheapest is the ________. That costs $________.

M How about the ________?

W The ________ is ________, but it takes the ____________ time.

M How ________ is it?

W It's $________ one way. The ____________ is $________.

C Listen and fill in the blanks.

W ________ you ________ an ________________ yet?

M No, I'm ____________, but I can't ____________.

W How ________ have you ________?

M ________. The ________ one was the ________ modern and the ____________.

W So?

M It's ________ the most ________________. The ____________ one is ____________, but the least ____________.

W And the ________?

M It's the ____________, but also the ____________.

W Hmm. They ________ have ________ and ________ points.

In the Neighborhood

KEY WORDS

Listen for these words and phrases.

neighbor	community	suburb	yard	porch
fire station	lawn	resident	considerate	barbecue

KEY EXPRESSIONS

Listen and match each question with its correct answer.

1. Do you know your neighbors? •	• (A) No. I'm going to meet him tomorrow.
2. What do you like about living in the suburbs? •	• (B) I know the upstairs neighbors. They're very friendly.
3. Do you have any problems with your neighbors? •	• (C) They're usually quiet, but sometimes they're very noisy.
4. Have you met your new neighbor yet? •	• (D) We see each other socially about once a month.
5. Do you ever get together with your neighbors? •	• (E) There are so many good things.

WARM-UP

TRACK 076

Listen and check what the speaker likes to do.

1. (A) Sit on the porch (B) Sit in the yard
2. (A) Mow the lawn (B) Plant flowers
3. (A) Fight fires (B) Cook
4. (A) Meet friends (B) Have barbecues
5. (A) Organize events (B) Visit communities

LISTEN FOR IT

TRACK 077

Listen and check the correct description of the speaker's neighbors.

1. (A) Considerate (B) Loud
2. (A) Friendly (B) Unkind
3. (A) New residents (B) Old residents
4. (A) Family members (B) School friends
5. (A) Nurses (B) Firefighters

TRUE OR FALSE

Listen and write T for true or F for false.

1. ______ (A) The speaker is going to her neighbor's house for dinner.
   ______ (B) The speaker's husband plays golf with their neighbor.

2. ______ (A) A model lives in apartment 102.
   ______ (B) Edward often listens to music.

3. ______ (A) The speaker does not get along with her neighbors and has a lot of problems.
   ______ (B) Someone was stealing things in her neighborhood.

LISTENING PRACTICE

TRACK 079

Listen and choose the correct answer.

1. What is this conversation mainly about?

   (A) The man's wife (B) The man's neighbors
   (C) The man's daughter (D) The man's job

2. Which of the following is NOT true?

   (A) The man enjoys spending time with his neighbors.
   (B) The man has no neighbors.
   (C) The man's neighbors have a child.
   (D) The man has a child.

3. What recent change occurred in the man's life?

   (A) He became a father.
   (B) He bought a house.
   (C) He moved to a new apartment.
   (D) He sold his house.

4. What complaint does the man have?

   (A) The woman is too loud.
   (B) His apartment has no hall.
   (C) His neighbor's child stole his jump rope.
   (D) His neighbors make a lot of noise.

5. How long has the man lived in his neighborhood?

   (A) One year (B) Two years
   (C) Three years (D) Four years

6. Which of the following is NOT an appropriate description of the man's neighbors?

   (A) Unfriendly (B) Considerate
   (C) Helpful (D) Kind

A Listen and fill in the blanks.

1. My __________ is so ________ at ________. I can't sleep well.
2. My neighbors __________ me to a __________ at their house every __________.
3. A __________ of four ________ into the ______________ next to mine ______________.
4. I live ________ ________ ________ my aunt, so I get to see my __________ almost every ________.
5. I ________ next to a ________ __________, so it can be very ________ at times.

B Listen and fill in the blanks.

W ________ you and your ________ ever get __________ with your ______________?

M We ________ each other __________ about once a ________. They ________ have us over for __________.

W That's ________. Do their __________ get ________ with your __________?

M Oh, yes. They have a __________ who's the ________ ________ as our Becky. They are in the ________ class at __________.

C Listen and fill in the blanks.

W How do you ________ your new ______________, Steve?

M It's ________. I've finally __________ some of my ______________.

W What are ________ like?

M The ______________ down the hall are ________ and __________. The family __________ are nice too, but ________. It's a __________ with two small children. One ________ likes to run and ________ a lot. The ________ is always __________ rope. ______________ they start at ________ a.m.

W Well, that's __________. They're just ________.

LISTENING TEST

TRACK 081

Listen and choose the correct answer.

1. What is the problem with the woman's new neighbors?
   (A) They're not quiet enough.
   (B) They get up too early.
   (C) Their dog is noisy.
   (D) The family is too big.

2. What does the woman find surprising about the family?
   (A) The four children are very quiet.
   (B) They have a lot of pets.
   (C) They never say hello.
   (D) They make a lot of noise at night.

3. Why does the man like sitting on his porch?
   (A) He can easily see his neighbors.
   (B) It's very quiet.
   (C) He can mow his lawn from there.
   (D) It's cool and shady.

4. Why does the woman think that the man is lucky?
   (A) He works at a hospital, like her.
   (B) He has good neighbors.
   (C) He has a nice family.
   (D) He can walk to work, unlike her.

5. What is the woman going to do soon?
   (A) Celebrate getting a new job
   (B) Cook a large meal
   (C) Hold a party for her brother
   (D) Get new neighbors

6. Why does the man think a potluck is a good idea?
   (A) The woman won't have to make a lot of food.
   (B) The woman will be able to make a lot of dishes herself.
   (C) It's a good way to meet new people.
   (D) He likes to try food made by other people.

DICTATION 2

A Listen and fill in the blanks.

M Have your _______ neighbors _______ in yet?

W Yes. They're _______, but there's already a _________.

M Are they _______?

W It's a _______ family. They have four children, but they're _____________ _______. The _________ is their _______.

M Oh, does it keep you _______ at _______?

W _______, but it gets me up _______ _______ with its _________.

M Hmm, you _______ have to get used to _________ up _______.

B Listen and fill in the blanks.

W _______ do you like about _________ in the _________, Dave?

M There are so many _______ _________. My _______ can play on the _______ in the _______ _______ while I sit on the _______ and relax. I see my _____________ all the time, and everyone _______ or stops to _______ when I'm sitting _________.

W Is there _________ negative about the _________?

M Not for me. I _______ at the local _______ _________, and it's only a ten-minute _______ from my house.

W Lucky you. I have to _______ for an _______ to get to work at the _________.

M Yeah, I think I'm pretty _______, and my _______ live near their _________, so it's good for all of _______.

C Listen and fill in the blanks.

M I _______ you're having a _______, Lisa.

W Yes, it's my brother's _________, and I want to have some _________ over for a small _____________.

M Will it be _________ only?

W No, we're _________ good _________ with our _____________ so they'll be coming too. It's going to be potluck, so _________ will bring some _______ or _______ to share.

M That's a _______ idea. It will make things much _________ for you.

W Yes, and _______ of my _____________ are really _______ cooks. Hey, why don't you _______? My _______ really likes you.

M I'd _______ to. What should I _______?

W How about some _______ of _________?

The Weather Forecast

KEY WORDS

TRACK 083

Listen for these words and phrases.

sunny	overcast	humid	chilly	snow
hail	drizzle	chance	lightning	heat wave

KEY EXPRESSIONS

Listen and match each question with its correct answer.

1. What's summer like in Seoul?
2. What's it like outside?
3. How was the weather in New York last spring?
4. Is it always this hot?
5. Is it supposed to rain a lot next week?

(A) It was cool and rainy.
(B) Summers tend to be hot and humid.
(C) No, it's going to be fairly dry.
(D) It's pouring rain.
(E) No, we're having a heat wave.

WARM-UP

TRACK 085

Listen and check what kind of weather the speaker is discussing.

1. (A) Spring weather (B) Winter weather
2. (A) Hail (B) Lightning
3. (A) Humid (B) Dry
4. (A) Overcast (B) Drizzle
5. (A) Humid (B) Sunny

LISTEN FOR IT

Listen and check what the weather was like yesterday.

1. (A) Humid (B) Hail
2. (A) Drizzle (B) Snow
3. (A) Cool (B) Cold
4. (A) Storm (B) Sunny
5. (A) Overcast (B) Heat wave

TRUE OR FALSE

Listen and write T for true or F for false.

1. ______ (A) The speaker is selling umbrellas.
   ______ (B) The umbrellas can only be used in the rain.

2. ______ (A) The woman went to Hawaii for a vacation.
   ______ (B) It didn't rain at all during Gail's vacation.

3. ______ (A) It is snowing outside.
   ______ (B) It will definitely rain tomorrow.

Listen and choose the correct answer.

1. Why is the woman complaining?
   (A) It's too wet.
   (B) It's too cold.
   (C) It's too dry.
   (D) It's too humid.

2. What does the woman want to do next week?
   (A) She wants to stay at home and watch TV.
   (B) She wants to dry her clothes outside.
   (C) She wants to go hiking.
   (D) She wants to meet the man.

3. Which of the following is NOT true about the man?
   (A) He lives in Canada.
   (B) He likes hot weather.
   (C) He is visiting the woman.
   (D) He wears shorts and a T-shirt in the summer.

4. What's the weather like now?
   (A) Cool
   (B) Sunny
   (C) Unusually hot
   (D) Unusually cool

5. What is the conversation mainly about?
   (A) The fashions in Korea
   (B) Winter weather in Korea
   (C) Business in Korea
   (D) Summer weather in Korea

6. Why did the man sweat a lot outdoors?
   (A) The weather was humid.
   (B) His clothes were too heavy.
   (C) The air conditioner in his office was broken.
   (D) He bought great suits.

A Listen and fill in the blanks.

1. Did you _______ the _______ _______________? It was as _______ as a baseball!
2. I _______ to take an ___________. It was only _______________, but I would have gotten _______ _______.
3. I ___________ Boston _______________, but it was much ___________ than I had ___________.
4. The ___________ was so _______ yesterday. My _______ hid under my _______!
5. It was so _______ yesterday— _______ ___________ than it usually is in _______.

B Listen and fill in the blanks.

W I'm _______ _______ with this ___________.

M _______? I ___________ you liked the _______.

W _______ this much! And I'm _______ _______ next week. Is it supposed to _______ a lot _______ _______?

M No, it's _______ to be fairly _______.

W _______. Maybe I'll be able to _______ ___________ during my _______ off. I really don't want to _______ my ___________ sitting at home ___________ TV.

M You know, it is ___________ to go ___________ in the _______.

W Yeah, I guess so. But it's _______ _______ when it's _______.

C Listen and fill in the blanks.

M Is it ___________ this _______? I'm dying of _______.

W No, we're having a _______ _______. It's usually around _______ °C, but this week it's _______°.

M I don't _______ how you can _______ here! I'm glad I'm only ___________.

W You _______ _______ _______ the heat when you _______ here. I mean, when I _______ you in Canada in the ___________, I feel kind of _______. When you are wearing ___________ and a T-shirt, I always _______ a sweater.

M Oh, that's true. You ___________ ask me to _______ off the _______ conditioning when you _______ me.

Listen and choose the correct answer.

1. What's the weather like?
   (A) Cloudy and snowy
   (B) Cold and cloudy
   (C) Fine but freezing
   (D) Cold and snowy

2. How does the man feel about lightning?
   (A) He thinks it is beautiful.
   (B) He thinks it is too loud.
   (C) He thinks it is scary.
   (D) He thinks it is enjoyable.

3. What is predicted for this weekend?
   (A) A thunderstorm
   (B) Warmer temperatures
   (C) Less wind
   (D) Hail

4. Which is NOT likely to be the temperature at the weekend?
   (A) 55°F
   (B) 62°F
   (C) 63°F
   (D) 71°F

5. What does the woman want to know about New York?
   (A) Fun things to do there in the spring
   (B) What the weather is like in spring
   (C) The cost of flights in the spring
   (D) Which hotel the man stayed at

6. Why does the man recommend visiting New York in spring?
   (A) The weather is not too hot and not too cold.
   (B) There is more to do in the spring.
   (C) There will be a lot of snow.
   (D) Air fares are cheaper in April.

DICTATION 2 TRACK 091

A Listen and fill in the blanks.

W The ________ is getting ____________ and darker.

M ________, and it's getting ________. I ________ a ________ is ____________.

W Is it supposed to ________ a lot ________?

M ________, and there ________ be some ____________ and ____________.

W We'd ____________ get ____________ before it starts ____________ rain.

M ________ idea. And you ________ how ____________ I am of ________________.

W Yes, I ________________ that ________ we were on the golf ____________ during a ________. You looked so ____________! But the ________ was so ________________.

B Listen and fill in the blanks.

M What's the ____________ ____________ for this ____________?

W The ____________ lady said it should be ____________, but there's a chance of ________.

M Do you ________ what the ________________ might be?

W ________ said we can ____________ lows in the mid-________s and highs in the low ________s.

M That doesn't ________ too ________. It's much better than the ________ we had ________________.

C Listen and fill in the blanks.

W I'm ____________ of ____________ New York. You've ________ there, haven't you, Tom?

M ________, I went there last ____________.

W How was the ____________ in New York last ____________? Is that a ________ ________ to go?

M It was ________, but the ____________ and ____________ were a little ________. The ________________ were nice. I was there in ________, but I think ________ would be ____________. ____________ is definitely better than ____________ for a trip. The ________ can get a lot of ________ in ____________, and the ____________ get really ________.

W OK, I'll ________ a ____________ for ________. I've always ____________ to go there.

Unit 11 My Day

KEY WORDS

Listen for these words and phrases.

do the laundry	vacuum	seldom	charge (a phone)	work out
make the bed	pick up (the kids)	buy groceries	take out the trash	shave

KEY EXPRESSIONS

TRACK 093

Listen and match each question with its correct answer.

1. Do you do any exercise?
2. Who does the laundry in your household?
3. How often do you vacuum your room?
4. Did you take the trash out?
5. Can I borrow your phone?

(A) I'm sorry. I completely forgot to do that.
(B) Yes, I work out every other day.
(C) Well, my wife washes clothes, but I wash the dishes.
(D) Did you forget to charge yours again?
(E) Not as often as I should.

WARM-UP TRACK 094

Listen and check what the speaker does on a typical day.

1. (A) Wash up before going to work (B) Clean the house before going to work
2. (A) Take the children to school (B) Get the children from school
3. (A) Make the bed in the morning (B) Make the bed at night
4. (A) Brush teeth once a day (B) Brush teeth twice a day
5. (A) Buy groceries (B) Go out for dinner

LISTEN FOR IT TRACK 095

Listen and check what the speaker did.

1. (A) Sent a text to his girlfriend (B) Forgot to charge his phone
2. (A) Vacuumed the house (B) Made a mess
3. (A) Had a small accident (B) Was late for work
4. (A) Worked out at a new gym (B) Took a class with a new trainer
5. (A) Wore a green shirt (B) Washed some clothes

TRUE OR FALSE

Listen and write T for true or F for false.

1. _______ (A) The man never has eggs for breakfast.
   _______ (B) The man drinks a lot of coffee.

2. _______ (A) The woman goes to bed around midnight.
   _______ (B) The woman has a TV in her bedroom.

3. _______ (A) The man does laundry every day.
   _______ (B) He has three children.

LISTENING PRACTICE

Listen and choose the correct answer.

1. Where is this conversation probably taking place?
   (A) At a hospital
   (B) In a house
   (C) At an office
   (D) In a taxi

2. What does the woman still need to do?
   (A) Brush her hair
   (B) Get dressed
   (C) Shave
   (D) Put on makeup

3. When should the boy take out the trash?
   (A) Every day
   (B) Tomorrow
   (C) Once a week
   (D) Never

4. Why doesn't the boy want to take out the trash now?
   (A) Because he is busy
   (B) Because he is tired
   (C) Because it is raining
   (D) Because he has to wash the dishes

5. Which of the following chores does the woman usually do?
   (A) Vacuuming
   (B) Cooking
   (C) Laundry
   (D) Dish washing

6. How does the man feel about the woman's family?
   (A) They are lazy.
   (B) They are selfish.
   (C) They are considerate.
   (D) They are unfriendly.

A Listen and fill in the blanks.

1. I ________ to ________ my cell ________ last night. I couldn't ________ to my girlfriend's texts, and now she is ________ at me.
2. I ________ the whole ________ before ________. But while I was out, my ________ made a big ________.
3. I ________ myself ________, so I had to go to ________ with a band aid on my ________.
4. I ________ ________ at the gym this ________. I also took a fitness ________ from a new trainer. Now I'm so ________.
5. I ________ to wear my ________ shirt, so I washed it this ________. But my ________ stopped ________, and I couldn't ________ the shirt after all.

B Listen and fill in the blanks.

W Are ________ in the ________, dear?

M Yes, I am. I'm ________. And then I need to ________ my ________.

W ________ you be much ________? I still need to ________ ________ my makeup.

M I'm ________ done. Just ________ me a ________.

W OK, but please ________. I don't want to be ________.

M I ________. ________ don't you ________ ________ ________ while you're waiting?

C Listen and fill in the blanks.

W Did you ________ ________ the ________, Mark?

M ________, Mom. I completely ________ about that. Can I do it ________?

W No, you ________ that you are supposed to do it ________ ________.

M ________ Mom, it's ________.

W Well, it wasn't ________ earlier. You should have ________ it out ________ it started to rain.

M This is so ________.

Listen and choose the correct answer.

1. What kind of exercise does the woman NOT do?

   (A) Golf
   (B) Walking
   (C) Weight training
   (D) Tennis

2. Why does the man cycle to work?

   (A) He had car troubles.
   (B) The subway is too expensive.
   (C) It's quicker than the subway.
   (D) He likes the exercise.

3. How long does the boy spend doing homework every evening?

   (A) 2 hours
   (B) 2 and a half hours
   (C) 4 hours
   (D) 6 and a half hours

4. Why doesn't the boy wash clothes?

   (A) He forgets to do it.
   (B) He is not good at it.
   (C) He doesn't like to do it.
   (D) He doesn't have a washing machine.

5. What does Tom want to do?

   (A) Charge his phone
   (B) Send a text
   (C) Receive a call
   (D) Use Jenny's phone

6. How often does Jenny call her parents?

   (A) Every day
   (B) Sometimes
   (C) Usually
   (D) Almost never

A Listen and fill in the blanks.

M ________ you do any ____________, Briana?

W Yes, I ________ ________ every other ________: usually weight lifting. And I ________ to ____________ every day.

M Do you ________ play ____________?

W Not anymore, but I took up ________ last ________. I'm getting quite ________. What about you, Chris? Are you into any ____________?

M Not really. But I ________ my ________ a lot. I used to ________ the ____________ to work, but it took about ________ ____________. If I ________ my ________, I can get to the ________________ in ________ minutes.

W That's convenient.

B Listen and fill in the blanks.

W ________ do you do every ____________?

M I come ________ from ____________ at 4:30. I usually do my ____________ until 6:30, and then I have ____________.

W Do you ever ____________ your ____________ cook dinner?

M Yes, ________________. But I can't make tasty ________ like my ________ does. I always ________ the ____________ after ____________.

W That's ________ of you. Who does the ____________ in your household?

M My ________. She says I don't get the ____________ clean ____________.

W ________ here. My mom ____________ all of my ____________.

C Listen and fill in the blanks.

M Can I ____________ your ________, Jenny?

W Sure. Did you ____________ to ____________ yours again, Tom?

M Yeah. And I have to ________ my ________ to let him know I'm about to ________.

W Do you ________ him every day?

M Yeah, he ________ ________ know ________ I am.

W I ____________ call my ________ and dad. But I do ________ ________.

M I think ________ people send ________, but my ________ always ________ me to call him. He says texts are for ________ ____________.

W And I guess he likes to ________ your ________.

M ________.

Unit 12 Let's Talk

KEY WORDS

Listen for these words and phrases.

telecommute	local call	international call	call back	put in one's contacts
caller ID	expect	video conference	service	text message

KEY EXPRESSIONS

Listen and match each question with its correct answer.

1. When do you expect her to get back?
2. May I have the number for Tom Leeds in Denver, Colorado?
3. Can I speak to your mother?
4. What telephone network do you use?
5. How do I make an international call?

(A) Yes, let me pass the phone to her.
(B) Well, first you'll need to enter the country code.
(C) Mobile Com. They have the best coverage.
(D) She should be back about 10:00.
(E) It's 515-739-0882.

WARM-UP TRACK 103

Listen and check what the speaker wants to do.

1. (A) Buy a new cell phone (B) Change to a new phone service
2. (A) Get someone's phone number (B) Give out his phone number
3. (A) Take a call in a quiet room (B) Take a nap in a quiet room
4. (A) Take an international flight (B) Make an international call
5. (A) Get the name of a shop (B) Get the phone number of a shop

LISTEN FOR IT TRACK 104

Listen and check why the speaker is calling.

1. (A) To reply to a message. (B) To return something to a store.
2. (A) To ask for an extension number (B) To speak to a particular person
3. (A) To inform Mary that he will be late (B) To invite Mary to dinner
4. (A) To find out about the availability of a product (B) To find out about the price of a product
5. (A) To ask a friend to call (B) To ask a friend to text him

TRUE OR FALSE TRACK 105

Listen and write T for true or F for false.

1. _______ (A) The speaker wants Bruce to call him back.
   _______ (B) Bruce may have to pay some money if he ignores this message.

2. _______ (A) Bill wants to speak to Mrs. Evans.
   _______ (B) Mrs. Evans will pass the phone to Marcy.

3. _______ (A) It is not possible to speak to someone immediately.
   _______ (B) This is a recorded message for a travel agency.

LISTENING PRACTICE

Listen and choose the correct answer.

1. What does the man want to do?
   (A) Make a collect call
   (B) Find out someone's telephone number
   (C) Make a call to another country
   (D) Make a local call

2. Why does the woman spell out the name?
   (A) Because the man speaks unclearly
   (B) To practice spelling
   (C) To avoid mistakes
   (D) Because the name is unusual

3. Who does the man want to call?
   (A) His Japanese teacher
   (B) A family he used to stay with
   (C) A Japanese restaurant
   (D) Lisa's family

4. Which of the following does the man NOT need?
   (A) A country code
   (B) An area code
   (C) A phone number
   (D) A pass code

5. When is Sandy expected back?
   (A) About 7:30
   (B) Tomorrow
   (C) In one hour
   (D) Around 10:00

6. What does Don say that he will do?
   (A) Call again tomorrow
   (B) Look for Sandy at the movie theater
   (C) See Sandy in math class
   (D) Call Sandy later tonight

DICTATION 1 TRACK 107

A Listen and fill in the blanks.

1. Hi, this is Brian Tanaka. I ________ your ____________, and I'm ________________ your ________.
2. Can I ________ to Anita Walker at ________________ 302?
3. Hi, Mary. It ________ like you can't ________ to the ________. I just wanted to let you ________ that I won't be ________ for ____________.
4. I'm ____________ about your advertisement on your ____________. Do you ________ have any of the ________ cakes ________?
5. Hey Amanda! ________ you get my ________? Call me ________! I need to ________ to you.

B Listen and fill in the blanks.

W Directory ________________.

M ________ I have the ____________ for ________ ____________ in Denver, Colorado?

W ____________ you. I'd like to ________ the ________. Is the last name ________-E-E-D?

M No, it's ________-E-E-D-S.

W I see. Just a ____________. The ____________ is 515-___ ___ ___-0882. May I ________ you with ____________ else?

M No. That's all, ________ you.

W ________ a ________ day.

C Listen and fill in the blanks.

M Hey, Lisa. I want to ________ my ________ homestay ____________ in ________. How do I ________ an ________________ ________? I've ________ done it ____________.

W That's ________. Well, ________ you'll need to ________ the country ________.

M OK, let me just ________ that ________... Got it. It's ________... No, it's ________ for Japan.

W So just ________ the country ________, then the ________ code. Then just call the ________ ____________.

M ________ sounds ________.

W It is! Just let me ________ if you have any ____________ getting ____________.

LISTENING TEST

Listen and choose the correct answer.

1. What is the relationship between Kevin and the second woman?
   (A) Friends
   (B) Husband and wife
   (C) Son and mother
   (D) Teacher and student

2. What does Helen mean when she says "You read my mind"?
   (A) She is reading the same book as Lisa.
   (B) She plans to read more.
   (C) She and Lisa both had the same idea.
   (D) She disagrees with Lisa's suggestion.

3. What is the woman's problem?
   (A) She doesn't get good cell phone service.
   (B) She needs a better cell phone.
   (C) She can't remember the password for her phone.
   (D) She forgot to pay her cell phone bill.

4. What does the woman think about the advertisements for Mobile Com?
   (A) They have great coverage.
   (B) They are annoying.
   (C) They are interesting.
   (D) They are boring.

5. What does You Jung like about her job?
   (A) She has great co-workers.
   (B) She has a lot of meetings.
   (C) Her commute is short.
   (D) She can work from home.

6. According to the woman, how do meetings held at the office compare to meetings held via teleconference?
   (A) They are similar.
   (B) They are longer.
   (C) They are shorter.
   (D) They are more difficult.

DICTATION 2 (TRACK 109)

A Listen and fill in the blanks.

M ________?

W1 Hello. Is that ________? This is Helen ________. Can I ________ to your ____________?

M Yes. Let me ________ the ________ to her… Mom! It's for ________!

W2 Hello?

W1 Hi, ________. It's Helen. Are you ________ ________? I have the ________ ________ work, and I ____________ it might be ________ to meet for ________.

W2 Definitely. Do you ________ to go to that ________ ________ on Broadway?

W1 You ________ my ________! Why don't I ________ you ________ at 11:30?

W2 I'll be ________!

B Listen and fill in the blanks.

W I'm ____________ to make a ________, but I can't get a ________ signal.

M ____________? I'm not ____________ any ____________. You have the ________ ________ of phone as me.

W The ____________ is not the ________. It's the ____________. I get really ________ ____________. I even have to pay ________ for caller ________. I ________ it. What ____________ company do you ________?

M Mobile Com. They have the ________ ____________.

W Hmm, I've ________ their advertisements. They ________ that really ____________ ________ promoting the ____________.

M He ________ be ____________, but the ____________ is good. You ____________ switch.

C Listen and fill in the blanks.

M How's your ________ ________ going, You Jung?

W It's ________. I ________ it. I telecommute ________ ________ a week, so it's very ______________.

M Isn't it ________________ to have ____________? I mean, you don't ________ much time in the ____________.

W Oh, that's not a ____________ at all. We use various ____________ ____________, and we do a lot of ________ conferences.

M Of ____________. But don't you find it ________________ to ________________ when you are not in the ________ ________ as your co-workers?

W Not really. And the ____________ are ____________ much ____________ than when we ________ at the ____________.

Transcripts

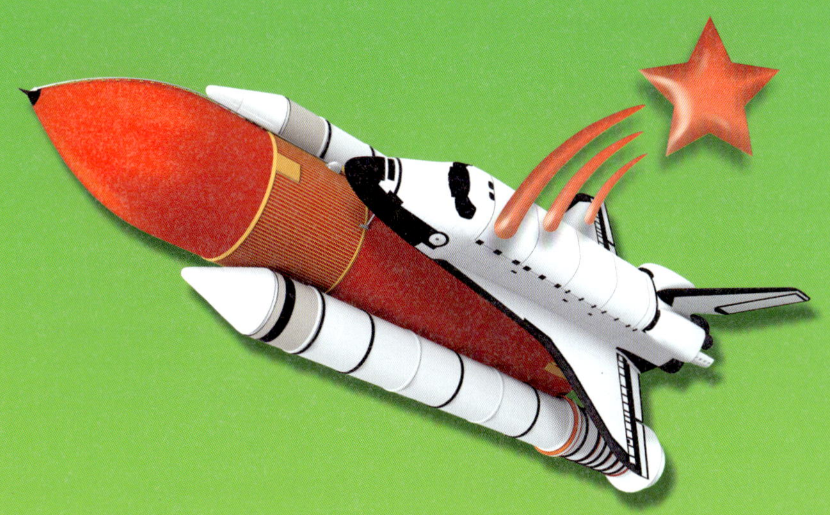

Unit 1 Tell Me About Yourself

KEY WORDS Track 002

Listen for these words and phrases.

address
nationality
zip code
hobby
spouse
occupation
first/last name
date of birth
gender
marital status

KEY EXPRESSIONS Track 003

Listen and match each question with its correct answer.

1. Where are you from?
2. Where do you live?
3. How old are you?
4. Where were you born?
5. What are your hobbies?

WARM-UP Track 004

Listen and check the correct information for the speaker.

1. What sports do you like?
2. What do you do in your free time?
3. How long have you lived here?
4. What do you do for a living?
5. What year were you born?

LISTEN FOR IT Track 005

Listen and check what kind of information is given.

1. **M** I met my wife when we were both students. We've been married for ten years. Her name is Lisa.
2. **W** My father is a very interesting man. He likes to golf, travel, and spend time with his children. His favorite hobby is probably taking pictures.
3. **W** I have too many numbers to remember! My telephone number, my apartment number, my social security number. But the most important is my PIN at the bank.
4. **M** My parents are originally from Florida, but they moved to California 13 years ago. We live on Market Street in San Francisco. Our apartment number is 302a.
5. **W** My name is Beth. I was born in France on May 25,1995. We moved to the United States when I was five years old.

TRUE OR FALSE Track 006

Listen and write T for true or F for false.

1. **W** Hello. My full name is Rachel Ann Lindstrom. I was born in Boston, Massachusetts, but live in Toronto, Canada now. I'm 28 years old, and I am an accountant. In my free time, I enjoy hiking, skiing, and listening to music.
2. **M** Hi. I'm Joe.
   W Hi.
   M Excuse me. What's your name?
   W I'm Jackie.
   M Do you live around here?
   W Yes, I live on Lakeside Avenue. I've lived there for six months. How about you?
   M I'm also on Lakeside Avenue.
3. **W** What do you like to do in your free time?
   M I like to do a lot of things. I enjoy reading and cooking food for my friends.
   W Do you like any sports?
   M Sure. I love to play tennis, swim, and do yoga.
   W You certainly are active!

LISTENING PRACTICE Track 007

Listen and choose the correct answer.

Questions 1 and 2 refer to the following dialog.

M Your résumé looks great, Ms. Parker. We just have one more question for you.
W Sure.
M I see you were born in Spain. Do you speak Spanish?
W Yes. I speak both English and Spanish fluently.
M Wonderful. We have a lot of customers who are Spanish speakers. We'll call you in the next couple of days with our decision.

Questions 3 and 4 refer to the following dialog.

M Hello. Are you Mrs. Lynne?
W Actually, Lynne is my first name. My family name is Webster. My husband is Ted Webster. He works in your office.
M Oh, of course. I'm sorry. I'm Kelly Madison.
W How do you do, Mr. Madison?
M How do you do? It's nice to meet you.

Questions 5 and 6 refer to the following dialog.

W Are you coming over for dinner tomorrow night?
M Yes. I can't wait to see your home. What time do you want me to get there?

W About seven. Do you have our address?
M I have your street address, 102 Wilshire Drive. Is that it?
W We're in Apartment 5. It's on the second floor. I'll text our address to you, just in case.
M Great. I'll see you tomorrow.

DICTATION 1 Track 008

A. Listen and fill in the blanks.

1. I met my wife when we were both students. We've been married for ten years. Her name is Lisa.
2. My father is a very interesting man. He likes to golf, travel, and spend time with his children. His favorite hobby is probably taking pictures.
3. I have too many numbers to remember! My telephone number, my apartment number, my social security number. But the most important is my PIN at the bank.
4. My parents are originally from Florida, but they moved to California 13 years ago. We live on Market Street in San Francisco. Our apartment number is 302a.
5. My name is Beth. I was born in France on May 25, 1995. We moved to the United States when I was five years old.

B. Listen and fill in the blanks.

M Your résumé looks great, Ms. Parker. We just have one more question for you.
W Thank you.
M I see you were born in Spain. Do you speak Spanish?
W Yes. I speak both English and Spanish fluently.
M Wonderful. We have a lot of customers who are Spanish speakers. We'll call you in the next couple of days with our decision.

C. Listen and fill in the blanks.

M Hello. Are you Mrs. Lynne?
W Actually, Lynne is my first name. My family name is Webster. My husband is Ted Webster. He works in your office.
M Oh, of course. I'm sorry. I'm Kelly Madison.
W How do you do, Mr. Madison?
M How do you do? It's nice to meet you.

LISTENING TEST Track 009

Listen and choose the correct answer.

Questions 1 and 2 refer to the following dialog.

M Excuse me. Could you help me a moment with this form?
W Sure.
M What does DOB mean?
W It means date of birth.
M Oh. And how about gender?
W That means, "Are you a man or a woman?" Just check 'M'.
M Thank you. I appreciate your help.
W It was my pleasure.

Questions 3 and 4 refer to the following dialog.

M OK. That completes your purchase. Do you want to take the table with you, or have it delivered?
W I'd like it delivered, please. How much will that cost?
M Delivery is free.
W Wonderful. I'd like it delivered to 3420 Golden State Drive, Anyville, California. And the zip code is 59302.
M Could you also give me a phone number?
W 665-4456.

Questions 5 and 6 refer to the following dialog.

W I'm afraid some information is missing from your visa application. Do you have your ID card with you?
M Yes, here it is.
W Oh, you were born in England?
M That's right. In Liverpool.
W Do you often go back to England?
M Not really. Most of my family live here in the US.
W Ah, I see.

DICTATION 2 Track 010

A. Listen and fill in the blanks.

M Excuse me. Could you help me a moment with this form?
W Sure.
M What does DOB mean?
W It means date of birth.
M Oh. And how about gender?
W That means, "Are you a man or a woman?" Just check 'M'.
M Thank you. I appreciate your help.
W It was my pleasure.

B. Listen and fill in the blanks.

M OK. That completes your purchase. Do you want to take the table with you, or have it delivered?

W I'd like it delivered, please. How much will that cost?
M Delivery is free.
W Wonderful. I'd like it delivered to 3420 Golden State Drive, Anyville, California. And the zip code is 59302.
M Could you also give me a phone number?
W 665-4456.

C. **Listen and fill in the blanks.**

M I'm afraid some information is missing from your visa application. Do you have your ID card with you?
M Yes, here it is.
W Oh, you were born in England?
M That's right. In Liverpool.
W Do you often go back to England?
M Not really. Most of my family live here in the US.
W Ah, I see.

Unit 2 Occupations

KEY WORDS Track 011

Listen for these words and phrases.

retired	unemployed
flight attendant	nurse
teacher	accountant
waiter/waitress	graphic designer
mechanic	bank teller

KEY EXPRESSIONS Track 012

Listen and match each question with its correct answer.

1. What do you do for a living?
2. Is the job still available?
3. How are you enjoying your new job?
4. What do you like about your job?
5. What do you do in a typical day?

WARM-UP Track 013

Listen and check the correct job for the speaker.

1. I help clients with their financial records and money.
2. I assist passengers on an airplane.
3. I create pictures and text for posters and magazines.
4. I fix cars when something's not working.
5. I turned 65 last year, so I had to stop working.

LISTEN FOR IT Track 014

Listen and check the speaker's occupation.

1. W I'm sorry, but you need to fasten your seat belt. The plane will be landing soon.
2. M I just need to take your temperature, and I'll get your pills.
3. W OK, here is $20, $40, $60, $80, $100. Is there anything else I can do for you today?
4. M I have the fish for you, sir. And who ordered the spaghetti?
5. W Please show me your driver's license. You were speeding, sir.

TRUE OR FALSE Track 015

Listen and write T for true or F for false.

1. M What do you do for a living?
W I work at a university.
M Oh, are you a professor?
W Actually, I'm a nurse in the health center there. What do you do?
M I'm a full-time student right now. I hope to be a graphic designer.

2. W Hello.
M Hello. I'm calling about the 'Help Wanted' ad in the paper.
W Do you mean the job for the part-time cashier?
M Yes, is the job still available?
W Yes. Do you have any experience as a cashier?
M Yes, I do. I worked at Smart Mart for six months.
W In that case, can you come in for an interview tomorrow at three?
M Yes, thank you. I'll be there.

3. M Sally, I think I'm going to quit my job.
W What? I thought you liked being a waiter.
M I like the money and the hours.
W Then what is the problem?
M It's my manager. We don't get along.
W What kind of job do you think you'll do next?
M I want to get a job at a different restaurant.

LISTENING PRACTICE Track 016

Listen and choose the correct answer.

Questions 1 and 2 refer to the following talk.

M I'm a university student and will graduate in a few months. I need to decide what I want to do after I graduate. My father is a doctor, and he wants me to be a doctor, too. But that would mean a lot more studying, and I don't think my grades are good enough. My mother is a teacher. She says I should do whatever I want to do. I'm interested in design and photography, so it might be fun to be a graphic designer. I'll travel for a few months, and then I will decide.

Questions 3 and 4 refer to the following talk.

W I did something that many people find strange. I was an architect for many years. It was a good job. The pay was high, but the hours were so long. So I quit about five years ago. I wanted to have my own business and be my own boss. I studied for a certificate in hair styling and opened a salon in my home. I have a lot of customers, and I can stay home. I love it, but people think I'm a little crazy.

Questions 5 and 6 refer to the following dialog.

M What do you like about your job?
W Well, I like my co-workers. The people I work with are very friendly.
M That's important. How about the job itself?
W I have a lot of freedom to make decisions for myself. My boss trusts me to do a good job.
M I want a job like that. My boss doesn't let me have any responsibility.
W Yes, but you only started a few weeks ago.

DICTATION 1 Track 017

A. Listen and fill in the blanks.

1. I'm sorry, but you need to fasten your seat belt. The plane will be landing soon.
2. I just need to take your temperature and I'll get your pills.
3. OK, here is $20, $40, $60, $80, $100. Is there anything else I can do for you today?
4. I have the fish for you, sir. And who ordered the spaghetti?
5. Please show me your driver's license. You were speeding, sir.

B. Listen and fill in the blanks.

I'm a university student and will graduate in a few months. I need to decide what I want to do after I graduate. My father is a doctor, and he wants me to be a doctor, too. But that would mean a lot more studying and I don't think my grades are good enough. My mother is a teacher. She says I should do whatever I want to do. I'm interested in design and photography, so it might be fun to be a graphic designer. I'll travel for a few months, and then I will decide.

C. Listen and fill in the blanks.

I did something that many people find strange. I was an architect for many years. It was a good job. The pay was high, but the hours were so long. So I quit about five years ago. I wanted to have my own business and be my own boss. I studied for a certificate in hair styling and opened a salon in my home. I have a lot of customers, and I can stay home. I love it, but people think I'm a little crazy.

LISTENING TEST Track 018

Listen and choose the correct answer.

Questions 1 and 2 refer to the following dialog.

W How are you enjoying your new job?
M It's going well so far.
W What do you do on an average day?
M Well, first, I meet the pilot and the other flight attendants. Then, we do safety checks.
W What happens after that?
M That's when it gets very busy! The passengers start to board, and I have to help them find their seats. And once we start to fly, it's even busier while I hand out food and drinks.

Questions 3 and 4 refer to the following dialog.

W How's life, Kenny? Are you taking your lunch break?
M Didn't you hear? I lost my job.
W Your teller job at the bank?
M Yes. I'm unemployed at the moment.
W I'm sorry to hear that.
M Not at all. I want to get into writing. Now I have the time.
W Are you going to get a website?
M Yes, and things look promising.
W Well, good luck, Kenny.

Questions 5 and 6 refer to the following dialog.

M I heard that you retired.
W Yes, after twenty years as a mechanic.
M Do you miss work at all?
W Sure, sometimes. But now I can work on my own car!
M That's true. Are you going to take up any hobbies?

W Actually, I'm going to start teaching a class on car repair at the community center once a month.
M Nice.

DICTATION 2 Track 019

A. Listen and fill in the blanks.

W How are you enjoying your new job?
M It's going well so far.
W What do you do on an average day?
M Well, first, I meet the pilot and the other flight attendants. Then, we do safety checks.
W What happens after that?
M That's when it gets very busy! The passengers start to board, and I have to help them find their seats. And once we start to fly, it's even busier while I hand out food and drinks.

B. Listen and fill in the blanks.

W How's life, Kenny? Are you taking your lunch break?
M Didn't you hear? I lost my job.
W Your teller job at the bank?
M Yes. I'm unemployed at the moment.
W I'm sorry to hear that.
M Not at all. I want to get into writing. Now I have the time.
W Are you going to get a website?
M Yes, and things look promising.
W Well, good luck, Kenny.

C. Listen and fill in the blanks.

M I heard that you retired.
W Yes, after twenty years as a mechanic.
M Do you miss work at all?
W Sure, sometimes. But now I can work on my own car!
M That's true. Are you going to take up any hobbies?
W Actually, I'm going to start teaching a class on car repair at the community center once a month.
M Nice.

Unit 3 Describing Things

KEY WORDS Track 020

Listen for these words and phrases.

sharp	comfortable
dirty	(be) made of
wood	(be) used for
square	round
rectangular	plastic

KEY EXPRESSIONS Track 021

Listen and match each question with its correct answer.

1. Can you guess what it is?
2. What does it look like?
3. Can you describe your glasses for me?
4. How was her dress?
5. What's that rectangular thing over there?

WARM-UP Track 022

Listen and check the correct object.

1. It's long, thin, and made of wood.
2. They're metal or plastic and used for drawing lines.
3. I wear them to help me see better, especially when I read.
4. It's a rectangular box with wheels, and it takes me to places if I pay money.
5. It's a round object that we can use to play some sports.

LISTEN FOR IT Track 023

Listen and check what the speaker is describing.

1. It's long and I wear it around my neck. I wear a thick one made of wool in the winter.
2. These are long and thin, and can be made of wood, plastic, or metal. They are used for eating.
3. We use these round metal objects to buy things, but they don't usually have a high value.
4. It's usually square or rectangular and is made of glass. Every house has many so that the light can come in.
5. It's soft and comfortable to sit on while you watch TV or read a book.

TRUE OR FALSE Track 024

Listen and write T for true or F for false.

1. **W** Have you seen Karl's new car?
   M Yeah. He took me for a ride in it.
   W Me, too. It was so comfortable. The seats are so soft.
   M Yes, but the inside is made of cheap plastic. And it has very small wheels. It looks very square, like a toy car.

W Oh, I thought it was kind of cute. I'm thinking of buying one myself.

2. **W** What are you making?
   M Don't you know? These are the four wooden legs here.
   W Is it a bed?
   M It's too small for that.
   W What's that rectangular thing over there?
   M That will be the table top. It will be made of glass.
   W Oh, I know. It will be a coffee table.
   M That's right.

3. **W** What's wrong?
   M None of these knives is sharp.
   W I don't like to have them too sharp because I'm afraid of cutting myself.
   M I can't even slice this tomato with these knives. And this one is brown! What happened to it? It should be silver!
   W Oh, that was my grandmother's knife. It reminds me of her.
   M This is impossible. I'm buying a new set of knives tomorrow.

LISTENING PRACTICE Track 025

Listen and choose the correct answer.

Questions 1 and 2 refer to the following talk.

M I had a quiet weekend. On Saturday, I was busy all day. I cleaned my house and washed all my dirty clothes. On Sunday, I painted my bedroom. It used to have brown walls. But brown is a sad color. So I painted it light green. Now it looks so clean and fresh. Green is a relaxing color, so I think I will sleep better now.

Questions 3 and 4 refer to the following dialog.

W Oh, no. I've wrapped all the presents. But I forgot to put labels on them.
M Well, maybe we can work out what everything is. How about this large square box?
W Um, I put Julie's sweater in a square box. How heavy is it?
M It's not at all heavy.
W OK, that's Julie's gift. Can you find a very hard box? Like something made of wood?
M This feels like wood.
W Great, that's a wooden box for Grandpa.
M This is easy. Let's keep going.

Questions 5 and 6 refer to the following dialog.

M I bought a gift for you.
W Oh, how exciting! What is it?
M Can you guess what it is? I will tell you that it is round.
W Hmm. Is it a cookie from the new bakery? Or a donut?
M No. You can't eat it. And it was expensive.
W Is it a plate? I broke a plate last week.
M No! It's made of metal, and you can wear it on your finger.
W Ah, I know!

DICTATION 1 Track 026

A. Listen and fill in the blanks.

1. It's long, and I wear it around my neck. I wear a thick one made of wool in the winter.
2. These are long and thin, and can be made of wood, plastic, or metal. They are used for eating.
3. We use these round metal objects to buy things, but they don't usually have a high value.
4. It's usually square or rectangular and is made of glass. Every house has many so that the light can come in.
5. It's soft and comfortable to sit on while you watch TV or read a book.

B. Listen and fill in the blanks.

I had a quiet weekend. On Saturday, I was busy all day. I cleaned my house and washed all my dirty clothes. On Sunday, I painted my bedroom. It used to have brown walls. But brown is a sad color, so I painted it light green. Now it looks so clean and fresh. Green is a relaxing color, so I think I will sleep better now.

C. Listen and fill in the blanks.

W Oh, no. I've wrapped all the presents. But I forgot to put labels on them.
M Well, maybe we can work out what everything is. How about this large square box?
W Um, I put Julie's sweater in a square box. How heavy is it?
M It's not at all heavy.
W OK, that's Julie's gift. Can you find a very hard box? Like something made of wood?
M This feels like wood.
W Great, that's a wooden box for Grandpa.
M This is easy. Let's keep going.

LISTENING TEST Track 027

Listen and choose the correct answer.

Questions 1 and 2 refer to the following dialog.

M How was your weekend, Jill?
W Great. I went to my sister's wedding.
M Oh yeah? How was it?
W It was small and private, but very pretty. My sister was so happy.
M How was her dress?
W It was nice. It wasn't traditional. It was light yellow and short, but very pretty.

Questions 3 and 4 refer to the following dialog.

W I left my glasses in here after my math class last week. Have you seen them?
M I found three pairs last week. And two pencil cases and a water bottle. Can you describe your glasses for me?
W Well, they are metal. Actually, they are red metal, with a silver line along the side. Do you have them?
M I have a pair of blue-and-white metal glasses and a pair of brown plastic glasses, but nothing that looks like yours.
W Oh, no. New glasses will be so expensive.
M I'm sorry. I just don't have them.

Questions 5 and 6 refer to the following dialog.

W Larry asked me to take a tie to his office. He spilled coffee on himself.
M How about this blue one? Or this purple-and-gray one is nice.
W No. He told me which tie he wants, but I can't find it.
M What does it look like? I'll help you look.
W It is yellow with red spots.
M He wants that tie? It's so ugly.
W I agree, but Larry likes it. He says it makes his eyes look green.

DICTATION 2 Track 028

A. Listen and fill in the blanks.

M How was your weekend, Jill?
W Great. I went to my sister's wedding.
M Oh yeah? How was it?
W It was small and private, but very pretty. My sister was so happy.
M How was her dress?
W It was nice. It wasn't traditional. It was light yellow and short, but very pretty.

B. Listen and fill in the blanks.

W I left my glasses in here after my math class last week. Have you seen them?
M I found three pairs last week. And two pencil cases and a water bottle. Can you describe your glasses for me?
W Well, they are metal. Actually, they are red metal, with a silver line along the side. Do you have them?
M I have a pair of blue metal glasses and a pair of red plastic glasses, but nothing that looks like yours.
W Oh, no. New glasses will be so expensive.
M I'm sorry. I just don't have them.

C. Listen and fill in the blanks.

W Larry asked me to take a tie to his office. He spilled coffee on himself.
M How about this blue one? Or this purple-and-gray one is nice.
W No. He told me which tie he wants, but I can't find it.
M What does it look like? I'll help you look.
W It is yellow with red spots.
M He wants that tie? It's so ugly.
W I agree, but Larry likes it. He says it makes his eyes look green.

Unit 4 Describing People

KEY WORDS Track 029

Listen for these words and phrases.

straight	curly
chin	forehead
in one's 20s	mustache
bald	slim
scar	height

KEY EXPRESSIONS Track 030

Listen and match each question with its correct answer.

1. What does she look like?
2. How did you get that scar?
3. Can you give me a description of what he looks like?
4. Do you want me to introduce you to my cousin Patty?
5. How was your date?

WARM-UP Track 031

Listen and check the words that describe the speaker.

1. My hair is a light yellow color.
2. My hair is long and straight, but I wish it were curly.
3. I will be ninety-two on my next birthday.
4. I am heavier than I should be, but I like food too much!
5. I have hair growing on my face, between the bottom of my nose and the top of my mouth.

LISTEN FOR IT Track 032

Listen and check the word that matches the speaker.

1. I cut my knee badly when I was ten, and you can still see where the injury was.
2. I'm losing all my hair, just like my father and grandfather did.
3. The hair on my chin is starting to get very long now.
4. My brother Ken is good-looking and wants to be a model.
5. My hair is full of bends and twists. It's hard to brush sometimes.

TRUE OR FALSE Track 033

Listen and write T for true or F for false.

1. **M** Hey, Becky.
   W Yes, Ralph?
   M Do you know that girl over there?
   W The one with the glasses?
   M No, the other one. With the wavy hair.
   W Sure. That's Kim Phillips.
   M She's pretty. Does she have a boyfriend?
   W Ralph! I don't know. Why don't you ask her?

2. **M** So, Miss James. You say you were robbed.
   W That's right, officer. Somebody stole my purse.
   M Did you see him clearly?
   W Oh yes.
   M Can you tell me what he looked like?
   W He was tall and thin, and had light brown hair. His eyes were blue.
   M And how old was he?
   W He was in his early 20s.

3. **W** Are you going to meet Mrs. Parker at the airport?
   M Yes, that's correct. Have you ever met her?
   W Sure. Haven't you?
   M No. What does she look like?
   W She's about 50, I guess, and quite overweight. She has curly gray hair, medium length.
   M That should do it.
   W She always has a sad expression on her face, too.

LISTENING PRACTICE Track 034

Listen and choose the correct answer.

Questions 1 and 2 refer to the following talk.

M Who was my favorite teacher in high school? That would be Mr. Madison, my math teacher. He was young—in his thirties, I suppose. He made math fun, you know. He was funny, always making us laugh. And he had really crazy hair. But he was really serious about his teaching and our learning. He helped us a lot after class when we needed it.

Questions 3 and 4 refer to the following announcement.

W Attention, shoppers. We have a lost child in the store. Please be on the lookout for a boy, aged four. His name is Sam, and he is wearing a red baseball cap and a green T-shirt. His hair is black and straight. He was last seen in the toy department. If you see this boy, please contact a clerk immediately.

Questions 5 and 6 refer to the following dialog.

W1 Ugh, I hate my hair. It's too straight.
W2 Are you kidding? I wish I had hair like yours. I've always wanted straight blond hair.
W1 No way. I love your curly red hair. And your forehead. It's a great shape for your hair.
W2 But my forehead is huge. That's why I always cover it with my hair.
W1 It's funny. We both hate our hair, but we both love each other's!
W2 I guess we both want something that we can't have.

DICTATION 1 Track 035

A. Listen and fill in the blanks.

1. I cut my knee badly when I was ten, and you can still see where the injury was.
2. I'm losing all my hair, just like my father and grandfather did.
3. The hair on my chin is starting to get very long now.

4. My brother Ken is good-looking and wants to be a model.
5. My hair is full of bends and twists. It's hard to brush sometimes.

B. Listen and fill in the blanks.

Who was my favorite teacher in high school? That would be Mr. Madison, my math teacher. He was young—in his thirties, I suppose. He made math fun, you know. He was funny, always making us laugh. And he had really crazy hair. But he was really serious about his teaching and our learning. He helped us a lot after class when we needed it.

C. Listen and fill in the blanks.

Attention, shoppers. We have a lost child in the store. Please be on the lookout for a boy, aged four. His name is Sam, and he is wearing a red baseball cap and a green T-shirt. His hair is black and straight. He was last seen in the toy department. If you see this boy, please contact a clerk immediately.

LISTENING TEST Track 036

Listen and choose the correct answer.

Questions 1 and 2 refer to the following dialog.

W You don't have a girlfriend, do you, Joe?
M Me? No. Why?
W Do you want me to introduce you to my cousin Patty?
M I don't know. I'm not looking for a girlfriend.
W Well, she is pretty. She has short black hair, blue eyes, and she is very tall.
M I don't care about that. What is she like?
W She is very sweet. She is smart, too, but kind of serious.
M OK. When can I meet her?

Questions 3 and 4 refer to the following dialog.

W I didn't know you had a large scar on your leg.
M This? Oh, yeah. I've had it for years.
W How did you get that scar?
M I fell off my bike.
W That's all? I thought it would be something like a shark bite. I mean—you surf a lot.
M Hey, I'm sorry if it's not an exciting story. It really hurt, you know!

Questions 5 and 6 refer to the following dialog.

M How was your date, Cindy?
W Great. Ben is so cute.
M You like him then?
W Oh, yes. He is tall, handsome, and has beautiful brown eyes.
M What did you talk about?
W He's very interesting. He can draw and paint, too, so he's really artistic.

DICTATION 2 Track 037

A. Listen and fill in the blanks.

W You don't have a girlfriend, do you, Joe?
M Me? No. Why?
W Do you want me to introduce you to my cousin Patty?
M I don't know. I'm not looking for a girlfriend.
W Well, she is pretty. She has short black hair, blue eyes, and she is very tall.
M I don't care about that. What is she like?
W She is very sweet. She is smart, too, but kind of serious.
M OK. When can I meet her?

B. Listen and fill in the blanks.

W I didn't know you had a large scar on your leg.
M This? Oh, yeah. I've had it for years.
W How did you get that scar?
M I fell off my bike. And I landed on a sharp stick.
W That's all? I thought it would be something like a shark bite. I mean—you surf a lot.
M Hey, I'm sorry if it's not an exciting story. It really hurt, you know!

C. Listen and fill in the blanks.

M How was your date, Cindy?
W Great. Ben is so cute.
M You like him then?
W Oh, yes. He is tall, handsome, and has beautiful brown eyes.
M What did you talk about?
W He's very interesting. He can draw and paint, too, so he's really artistic.

Unit 5 Finding Places

KEY WORDS Track 038

Listen for these words and phrases.

kitty corner to	avenue
across from	behind
in front of	on the corner
block	turn left/right
intersection	traffic light

KEY EXPRESSIONS Track 039

Listen and match each question with its correct answer.

1. Can you tell me how to get there?
2. Do you know the street address?
3. Is there a supermarket near here?
4. Can I walk there from here?
5. Where are you now?

WARM-UP Track 040

Listen and check where the hotel is located.

1. The hotel is across from the park.
2. The hotel isn't next to the bank.
3. The post office is behind the hotel.
4. The hotel is over there, kitty corner to the supermarket.
5. To the right of the school, there's a hotel.

LISTEN FOR IT Track 041

Listen and check what the speaker says to do.

1. Turn right at the first traffic light.
2. Go east for three blocks.
3. Walk until you come to the third street.
4. Take a left after you pass the library.
5. Go up Lake Avenue until you see a church.

TRUE OR FALSE Track 042

Listen and write T for true or F for false.

1. W Tom, do you know where Shelly's apartment is?
   M Yes, it's kitty corner to the high school.
   W Do you know the street address?
   M She lives at 106 Bedford Road.
   W Can you tell me how to get there?
   M This is 11th Avenue, right? Just go straight until you get to Bedford. It's not far.

2. M Excuse me. Do you know where the post office is?
   W Sure. It's on 12th Street.
   M Can I walk there from here?
   W No, it's too far. You'll have to take a bus.
   M Do you know which one?
   W Take the 33 and get off at the corner of 12th and Simpson.
   M Thanks for your help.

3. M Is there a supermarket near here?
   W Not in this area. There's a convenience store down the street, though.
   M Which way is that?
   W Just follow this street until you see National Bank. It's just past that.
   M How far is it?
   W It's about five minutes on foot.
   M Great. Thank you.

LISTENING PRACTICE Track 043

Listen and choose the correct answer.

Questions 1 and 2 refer to the following talk.

W I'll give you directions to get to my house. Listen carefully, or write them down. The address is 1680 Lincoln Way. Got that? 1680 Lincoln Way. Take Second Avenue—it's the fastest route. Go straight until you come to the intersection of Second Avenue and Henderson Street. There, take a left, go straight for another six blocks, and you'll come to Lincoln Way. Turn right, and look for a blue house.

Questions 3 and 4 refer to the following talk.

M John, this is Cameron. Text me when you get this message. There's a party tomorrow at Mark and Edward's place. Do you know where they live? It's on Lexington Avenue. From your place, go east on Lexington until you come to Jameson Foods. They live behind there. Park your car at the store, and look for a white apartment building with blue stripes. They live in apartment 6B. Hope to see you around 7:00.

Questions 5 and 6 refer to the following dialog.

W Wait, did the man say to go left at the traffic light?
M No, he said to go right. Then go left just after we pass the bank.
W Oh, yes. I remember. That must be the traffic light.
M OK, so keep an eye out for the bank.
W I can see it. Oh, no. There is a bank on both sides of the street.
M Hmm, well, let's just go right by the bank on the right-hand side of the street.
W You know what? I'm just going to check a map on my phone. I don't want to get really lost.

DICTATION 1 Track 044

A. Listen and fill in the blanks.

1. Turn right at the first traffic light.
2. Go east for three blocks.
3. Walk until you come to the third street.

4. Take a left after you pass the library.
5. Go up Lake Avenue until you see a church.

B. Listen and fill in the blanks.

I'll give you directions to get to my house. Listen carefully, or write them down. The address is 1680 Lincoln Way. Got that? 1680 Lincoln Way. Take Second Avenue—it's the fastest route. Go straight until you come to the intersection of Second Avenue and Henderson Street. There, take a left, go straight for another six blocks, and you'll come to Lincoln Way. Turn right, and look for a blue house.

C. Listen and fill in the blanks.

John, this is Cameron. Text me when you get this message. There's a party tomorrow at Mark and Edward's place. Do you know where they live? It's on Lexington Avenue. From your place, go east on Lexington until you come to Jameson Foods. They live behind there. Park your car at the store, and look for a white apartment building with blue stripes. They live in apartment 6B. Hope to see you around 7.

LISTENING TEST Track 045

Listen and choose the correct answer.

Questions 1 and 2 refer to the following dialog.

W Excuse me. Is there a bookstore around here?
M Yes, there's one on Davis Street.
W And where is that?
M Oh, go up this street. This is Mayfair Lane. Take it up to the traffic light.
W Yes . . .
M Take a right, and go one block. That's Davis.
W OK . . .
M You'll see a large sporting goods store. The bookstore's above that.
W Thank you very much.

Questions 3 and 4 refer to the following dialog.

M Excuse me, but is this the way to the police station?
W No. It's not in this area.
M Isn't this Second Avenue?
W Sorry, this is Second Street.
M Oh, no. Where is Second Avenue?
W It's about eight blocks south of here.
M I see. Thanks.

Questions 5 and 6 refer to the following dialog.

W Hello.
M Hey Mary! It's Andrew. I can't find your apartment.
W Where are you now?
M I'm at the corner of McGregor and Park.
W You're close. Just walk east for a few minutes. You'll see a men's clothing store on the corner. Keep going straight, and cross the crosswalk. I'm the first door on the left.
M Got it. See you soon.

DICTATION 2 Track 046

A. Listen and fill in the blanks.

W Excuse me. Is there a bookstore around here?
M Yes, there's one on Davis Street.
W And where is that?
M Oh, go up this street. This is Mayfair Lane. Take it up to the traffic light.
W Yes . . .
M Take a right, and go one block. That's Davis.
W OK . . .
M You'll see a large sporting goods store. The bookstore's above that.
W Thank you very much.

B. Listen and fill in the blanks.

M Excuse me, but is this the way to the police station?
W No. It's not in this area.
M Isn't this Second Avenue?
W Sorry, this is Second Street.
M Oh, no. Where is Second Avenue?
W It's about eight blocks south of here.
M I see. Thanks.

C. Listen and fill in the blanks.

W Hello.
M Hey, Mary! It's Andrew. I can't find your apartment.
W Where are you now?
M I'm at the corner of McGregor and Park.
W You're close. Just walk east for a few minutes. You'll see a men's clothing store on the corner. Keep going straight, and cross the crosswalk. I'm the first door on the left.
M Got it. See you soon.

Unit 6 Making Plans

KEY WORDS Track 047

Listen for these words and phrases.

definitely	probably
predict	in (an hour / a week)
possible	plan
someday	might
promise	hope

KEY EXPRESSIONS Track 048

Listen and match each question with its correct answer.

1. What are you going to do after you graduate?
2. What are you doing this weekend?
3. What are your summer plans?
4. Have you made any New Year's resolutions?
5. What do you think you'll be doing thirty years from now?

WARM-UP Track 049

Listen and check the correct time expression.

1. I'll see you in a few minutes.
2. Call me at exactly a quarter to six.
3. Beatrice hopes to graduate soon.
4. Ted will turn 18 the year after next.
5. I'll be able to buy that watch someday.

LISTEN FOR IT Track 050

Listen and check what will probably happen next.

1. Angela, Susan wants you to call her right away.
2. Waiter, may we see the dessert menu?
3. Look, Bob. You got a warning letter from the gas company. You have to pay the bill immediately.
4. Get your money ready. Here comes the bus.
5. I like this jacket. Do you think it will fit me?

TRUE OR FALSE Track 051

Listen and write T for true or F for false.

1. W What are you doing this weekend, Stan?
   M I'm meeting my sister on Saturday at the airport.
   W The one who lives in Seattle?
   M Yes. She's coming to town with her son, my nephew. I'm going to take them to a baseball game and the zoo.
   W That sounds fun. I hope you have a great time together.
2. W I can't believe I just took my last exam.
   M Congratulations. What are you going to do after you graduate?
   W I have no idea what I want to do with my life.
   M You really have no idea?
   W I want to get a job in television. Maybe as a writer. But first, my friend Cara and I are going to take a trip. I want to have fun first.
   M Where are you going?
   W We're going to Mexico for a month.
3. M Happy New Year, Alice.
   W Thanks, Daniel.
   M Have you made any new year's resolutions?
   W Of course. I want to lose some weight and learn Spanish.
   M Learn Spanish? Why?
   W I don't know. Maybe I'll travel to Spain or something.
   M I'm planning to read more books and to get more exercise.
   W Well, good luck.
   M You, too.

LISTENING PRACTICE Track 052

Listen and choose the correct answer.

Questions 1 and 2 refer to the following talk.

W People ask me what I want to do in the future. That's a difficult question to answer. I'll graduate next year, when I'm 22, so I need to make some decisions. I won't go to graduate school next year. But I will go eventually. I know that for sure. I want to get a job in the computer industry. I'll definitely get married someday, but I don't know when. It's possible that I will have children. But I'm not sure. I like kids, but want to have a career. I'll decide that with my husband.

Questions 3 and 4 refer to the following talk.

W Excuse me, Doctor Lynne? Could we go over your schedule for today? As you know, I will be leaving a little early today. You have four appointments with patients this morning, from 10 to 12:30. At 12:30, Dr. Carrington will be stopping by to discuss some things. You have a meeting at 1:00, and that should last for about half an hour. For the rest of the day, you can see you will be pretty free. I'll be here until 3:30 to answer any calls.

Questions 5 and 6 refer to the following dialog.

W What do you think you'll be doing thirty years from now?

M I'll probably be working in an office. Maybe getting ready to retire. And I'll probably go for walks in the park on the weekends.

W That's kind of dull.

M But realistic. How about you?

W I predict we will all be living on Mars by then. So I'll probably own a business on Mars.

M Yeah, I'm sure that is not going to happen.

DICTATION 1 Track 053

A. Listen and fill in the blanks.

1. Angela, Susan wants you to call her right away.
2. Waiter, may we see the dessert menu?
3. Look, Bob. You got a warning letter from the gas company. You have to pay the bill immediately.
4. Get your money ready. Here comes the bus.
5. I like this jacket. Do you think it will fit me?

B. Listen and fill in the blanks.

People ask me what I want to do in the future. That's a difficult question to answer. I'll graduate next year, when I'm 22, so I need to make some decisions. I won't go to graduate school next year. But I will go eventually. I know that for sure. I want to get a job in the computer industry. I'll definitely get married someday, but I don't know when. It's possible that I will have children. But I'm not sure. I like kids, but want to have a career. I'll decide that with my husband.

C. Listen and fill in the blanks.

Excuse me, Doctor Lynne? Could we go over your schedule for today? As you know, I will be leaving a little early today. You have four appointments with patients this morning, from 10 to 12:30. At 12:30, Dr. Carrington will be stopping by to discuss some things. You have a meeting at 1:00, and that should last for about half an hour. For the rest of the day, you can see you will be pretty free. I'll be here until 3:30 to answer any calls.

LISTENING TEST Track 054

Listen and choose the correct answer.

Questions 1 and 2 refer to the following dialog.

M What are your summer plans, Megan?

W Well, I'm going to summer school in July and then going to Dallas.

M Dallas? Why are you going there?

W My friend is getting married on August 5th, so I'll attend her wedding.

M And after that?

W I'll visit my parents for a week and then return home.

M That sounds like a good summer.

Questions 3 and 4 refer to the following dialog.

M Do you want to get together on Friday?

W What time?

M I'm meeting Greg at 5:00. Join us then.

W I can't. I have to work till 6:00.

M Meet us later for dinner then.

W OK. How about 7:30?

M Sounds good. Come to the Vega Café.

W I'll be there.

Questions 5 and 6 refer to the following talk.

M Sometimes I feel very worried about the future. Humans do so many things that harm the Earth. My friends drive everywhere. I'm trying to persuade them to walk, ride bicycles, or use public transportation. I predict that if we all stop using cars at least one day a week, the air will be much less polluted. Why don't you try?

DICTATION 2 Track 055

A. Listen and fill in the blanks.

M What are your summer plans, Megan?

W Well, I'm going to summer school in July and then going to Dallas.

M Dallas? Why are you going there?

W My friend is getting married on August 5th, so I'll attend her wedding.

M And after that?

W I'll visit my parents for a week and then return home.

M That sounds like a good summer.

B. Listen and fill in the blanks.

M Do you want to get together on Friday?

W What time?

M I'm meeting Greg at 5:00. Join us then.

W I can't. I have to work till 6:00.

M Meet us later for dinner then.

W OK. How about 7:30?

M Sounds good. Come to the Vega Café.

W I'll be there.

C. Listen and fill in the blanks.

Sometimes I feel very worried about the future. Humans do so many things that harm the Earth. My friends drive everywhere. I'm trying to persuade them to walk, ride bicycles, or use public transportation. I predict that if we all stop using cars at least one day a week, the air will be much less polluted. Why don't you try?

Unit 7 In the Past

KEY WORDS Track 056

Listen for these words and phrases.

last	ago
since	previous
remember	memory
childhood	used to
experience	made

KEY EXPRESSIONS Track 057

Listen and match each question with its correct answer.

1. Do you remember Grandma's house?
2. Did you see Laura last night?
3. Where have you been?
4. What is your earliest memory?
5. How was your trip?

WARM-UP Track 058

Listen and check the correct time expressions.

1. Kerry got married seven days ago.
2. I started this job the year before last.
3. They've lived in Germany for a couple of years.
4. The movie started at 7:45.
5. Bradley got to the meeting in time.

LISTEN FOR IT Track 059

Listen and check what probably just happened.

1. Did you hear that, Roseanne? Can you get the door please?
2. I left some room for a sweet treat. May we please see the dessert menu?
3. I feel so much cleaner now.
4. I'm glad we landed on time. But we need to go through Customs and Immigration now.
5. David, it was so nice of you. The sweater fits perfectly.

TRUE OR FALSE Track 060

Listen and write T for true or F for false.

1. **M** Did you see Laura last night?
   W No, we got together night before last. I was studying last night.
   M What did the two of you do?
   W We had dinner in that new restaurant on Elm Avenue.
   M How was it?
   W Not so good, actually. It was pretty expensive, but the food wasn't great.

2. **W** Do you remember Grandma's house?
   M Of course. I have lots of good memories of her house.
   W Do you remember when we hid in her closet?
   M Yes, and she couldn't find us. So she thought we had run away.
   W And she searched for us in the streets around the house.
   M But we'd fallen asleep in the closet.
   W She was so angry when she found us. But she couldn't stay mad! I miss her.

3. **W** Where have you been?
   M I was at Terry's house.
   W Why didn't you go to basketball?
   M I did, but after basketball practice I went to his house to work on some homework.
   W You should have called or texted me. I was worried.
   M Sorry, Mom. It was thoughtless of me.
   W Yes, it was. Don't do it again.

LISTENING PRACTICE Track 061

Listen and choose the correct answer.

Questions 1 and 2 refer to the following talk.

W Thank you for considering me for the job, sir. I graduated from university in 2010 with a degree in finance. I started work the same year as a manager for Wilson Jewelers. I worked there for 2 years, and then I returned to graduate school. I got my master's degree in business administration in 2014. Since then, I have been working as the China regional sales manager at Semtex Corporation. I have a proven record of sales, and I have established accounts worth over $34 million this year alone. My previous experience makes me ideal for this position.

Questions 3 and 4 refer to the following talk.

M I had a good childhood. I am the youngest of four children. I have two older brothers and a sister. We often played together as kids. We used to play basketball, football, and go swimming every summer. It seems like I was never alone. Until I was 12, we lived in the countryside, but then my father got a new job so we moved to a city. Suddenly, we were living in an apartment on the 20th floor. None of us liked it very much.

Questions 5 and 6 refer to the following dialog.

M Jane, what is your earliest memory?
W Umm, maybe when my sister was born. I was four, and I remember my parents bringing her home. How about you?
M I can remember my first day of school. It was really cold.
W I remember my first day of school, too. I didn't want to go, and I cried so much.
M Oh, I really wanted to go. I ran all the way there, and my poor mom had to run behind me.
W Yes, I remember you always did like school.

DICTATION 1 Track 062

A. Listen and fill in the blanks.

1. Did you hear that, Roseanne? Can you get the door, please?
2. I left some room for a sweet treat. May we please see the dessert menu?
3. I feel so much cleaner now.
4. I'm glad we landed on time. But we need to go through Customs and Immigration now.
5. David, it was so nice of you. The sweater fits perfectly.

B. Listen and fill in the blanks.

Thank you for considering me for the job, sir. I graduated from university in 2010 with a degree in finance. I started work the same year as a manager for Wilson Jewelers. I worked there for 2 years, and then I returned to graduate school. I got my master's degree in business administration in 2014. Since then, I have been working as the China regional sales manager at Semtex Corporation. I have a proven record of sales, and I have established accounts worth over $34 million this year alone. My previous experience makes me ideal for this position.

C. Listen and fill in the blanks.

I had a good childhood. I am the youngest of four children. I have two older brothers and a sister. We often played together as kids. We used to play basketball, football, and go swimming every summer. It seems like I was never alone. Until I was 12, we lived in the countryside, but then my father got a new job, so we moved to a city. Suddenly, we were living in an apartment on the 20th floor. None of us liked it very much.

LISTENING TEST Track 063

Listen and choose the correct answer.

Questions 1 and 2 refer to the following dialog.

W Hey, George. I tried to call and text you last night. Why didn't you answer?
M Sorry. I was feeling really sick last night, so I turned off my phone and went to bed early.
W Are you OK now?
M I guess, but I still have a bit of a fever and my head really hurts.
W I'm sorry to hear that. Can I get anything for you?
M No, I'm just going to go home again after this meeting. I have to give a sales report. Then I'm going back to bed.

Questions 3 and 4 refer to the following dialog.

M Welcome home. How was your trip?
W Great.
M Where did you go, again?
W We took a bus tour in Australia.
M That's right. Did you stay mostly in Sydney or did you travel around?
W We went all over. Like I said, it was a bus trip.
M How was the accommodation?
W We usually stayed in hotels, but sometimes we went camping or stayed in small private inns.

Questions 5 and 6 refer to the following dialog.

M Happy birthday, Mom.
W Oh, Billy. Thank you. What a surprise!
M Look. I cooked you breakfast and Susan cleaned up the kitchen.
W How sweet of you two!
M I made bacon and eggs, orange juice, toast, and coffee.
W It looks delicious. Thanks again.

DICTATION 2 Track 064

A. Listen and fill in the blanks.

W Hey, George. I tried to call and text you last night. Why didn't you answer?
M Sorry. I was feeling really sick last night, so I turned off my phone and went to bed early.
W Are you OK now?
M I guess, but I still have a bit of a fever and my head really hurts.
W I'm sorry to hear that. Can I get anything for you?
M No, I'm just going to go home again after this meeting. I have to give a sales report. Then I'm going back to bed.

B. Listen and fill in the blanks.

M Welcome home. How was your trip?
W Great.
M Where did you go, again?
W We took a bus tour in Australia.
M That's right. Did you stay mostly in Sydney or did you travel around?
W We went all over. Like I said, it was a bus trip.
M How was the accommodation?
W We usually stayed in hotels, but sometimes we went camping or stayed in small private inns.

C. Listen and fill in the blanks.

M Happy birthday, Mom.
W Oh, Billy. Thank you. What a surprise!
M Look. I cooked you breakfast, and Susan cleaned up the kitchen.
W How sweet of you two!
M I made bacon and eggs, orange juice, toast, and coffee.
W It looks delicious. Thanks again.

Unit 8 Making Comparisons

KEY WORDS Track 065

Listen for these words.

better	worse
more	less
least	happier
modern	popular
wetter	easiest

KEY EXPRESSIONS Track 066

Listen and match each question with its correct answer.

1. Which city did you like more?
2. Which jacket is better quality?
3. What's the best way to go downtown?
4. Is the bus quicker than the subway?
5. Which hotel will you be staying at in Hong Kong?

WARM-UP Track 067

Listen and check the correct information.

1. Bill is 54 years old, and Paul is 45.
2. Bill weighs 78 kilos, and Paul weighs 77.
3. Bill isn't as rich as Paul.
4. Bill has one fewer child than Paul.
5. Bill has many more friends than Paul does.

LISTEN FOR IT Track 068

Listen and check the correct information.

1. It rains more in Seattle than in London.
2. Becky sings much better than Jill.
3. On the test, Ron got a C, but Joe got an A.
4. The blue car isn't as expensive as the white one.
5. Mr. Lee works 10 hours more per week than Mr. Kim does.

TRUE OR FALSE Track 069

Listen and write T for true or F for false.

1. **M** Hi Linda. Where have you been?
W I just saw the movie *Road Chase II*.
M Oh, yes? How was it?
W I liked *Road Chase I* better.
M Why?
W It was more exciting. *Road Chase II* wasn't as interesting. Also, the first movie was shorter. This one was just too long.

2. **W** How was your trip to Europe?
M Amazing. I loved London and Paris.
W Which city did you like more?
M I think London was better.
W Why?
M The nightlife was more interesting, and the people seemed friendlier.
W So you didn't like Paris?
M I liked it, but for different reasons. The food was much better there.

3. **W** Which of these two jackets should we buy for Samantha?
M I don't know. The black one is prettier.
W Yes, but it's also more expensive.
M Which jacket is better quality?
W I think the red one is a bit better. It feels heavier and is better made.
M You're right. Let's get it.

LISTENING PRACTICE Track 070

Listen and choose the correct answer.

Questions 1 and 2 refer to the following talk.

W I have three wonderful children. The oldest, Beth, will be in college next year. Next is Danny, who is 15, and then 12-year-old Peter. Danny is the most athletic. Peter likes some sports, but Beth doesn't play any sports at all. She loves music and can sing well and play several musical instruments. Peter seems interested in music, but we'll see. Danny isn't musical at all. All three are smart, and I wouldn't dare say which one I think is the smartest.

Questions 3 and 4 refer to the following talk.

M I like school a lot. My favorite subject is science. I find it the most interesting, but also the most difficult. I usually get Bs in that class. The easiest class by far is English. P.E. is the most fun—I love playing sports. I find math class pretty boring, but not nearly as boring as history. That's the worst.

Questions 5 and 6 refer to the following dialog.

W What's the best way to go downtown? Parking is so difficult these days.
M Probably the bus. It stops at a lot of places in the city center.
W Is the bus quicker than the subway?
M I'd say they both take the same time.
W Well, is it cheaper?
M No, they both cost $1.75. I prefer the bus because it is less crowded and you can see where you are going.

DICTATION 1 Track 071

A. Listen and fill in the blanks.

1. It rains more in Seattle than in London.
2. Becky sings much better than Jill.
3. On the test, Ron got a C, but Joe got an A.
4. The blue car isn't as expensive as the white one.
5. Mr. Lee works 10 hours more per week than Mr. Kim does.

B. Listen and fill in the blanks.

I have three wonderful children. The oldest, Beth, will be in college next year. Next is Danny, who is 15, and then 12-year-old Peter. Danny is the most athletic. Peter likes some sports, but Beth doesn't play any sports at all. She loves music and can sing well and play several musical instruments. Peter seems interested in music, but we'll see. Danny isn't musical at all. All three are smart, and I wouldn't dare say which one I think is the smartest.

C. Listen and fill in the blanks.

I like school a lot. My favorite subject is science. I find it the most interesting, but also the most difficult. I usually get Bs in that class. The easiest class by far is English. P.E. is the most fun—I love playing sports. I find math class pretty boring, but not nearly as boring as history. That's the worst.

LISTENING TEST Track 072

Listen and choose the correct answer.

Questions 1 and 2 refer to the following dialog.

M Which hotel will you be staying at in Hong Kong?
W I don't know yet.
M The St. George is the most convenient, but of course, is the most expensive.
W How about the Park Lane?
M It's cheap, yes, but not as cheap as the Crown Royal if you want to save money.
W Yes, but the Crown Royal is so inconvenient. It's the farthest from all the places that I want to visit.

Questions 3 and 4 refer to the following dialog.

W May I help you?
M Yes, how can I get from Vienna to Budapest?
W Well, you have four choices—train, bus, boat, or air.
M Which is the cheapest?
W Bus. There are tickets from $12. The second cheapest is the train. That costs $58.
M How about the boat?
W The boat is nice, but it takes the longest time.
M How much is it?
W It's $100 one way. The flight is $190.

Questions 5 and 6 refer to the following dialog.

W Have you found an apartment yet?
M No, I'm looking, but I can't decide.
W How many have you seen?
M Three. The first one was the most modern and the biggest.
W So?
M It's also the most expensive. The second one is cheaper, but the least modern.
W And the third?
M It's the cheapest, but also the smallest.
W Hmm. They all have good and bad points.

DICTATION 2 Track 073

A. Listen and fill in the blanks.

M Which hotel will you be staying at in Hong Kong?
W I don't know yet.
M The St. George is the most convenient, but of course is the most expensive.
W How about the Park Lane?
M It's cheap, yes, but not as cheap as the Crown Royal if you want to save money.
W Yes, but the Crown Royal is so inconvenient. It's the farthest from all the places that I want to visit.

B. Listen and fill in the blanks.

W May I help you?
M Yes, how can I get from Vienna to Budapest?
W Well, you have four choices—train, bus, boat, or air.
M Which is the cheapest?
W Bus. There are tickets from $12. The second cheapest is the train. That costs $58.
M How about the boat?
W The boat is nice, but it takes the longest time.
M How much is it?
W It's $100 dollars one way. The flight is $190.

C. Listen and fill in the blanks.

W Have you found an apartment yet?
M No, I'm looking, but I can't decide.
W How many have you seen?
M Three. The first one was the most modern and the biggest.
W So?
M It's also the most expensive. The second one is cheaper, but the least modern.
W And the third?
M It's the cheapest, but also the smallest.
W Hmm. They all have good and bad points.

Unit 9 In the Neighborhood

KEY WORDS Track 074

Listen for these words and phrases.

neighbor	community
suburb	yard
porch	fire station
lawn	resident
considerate	barbecue

KEY EXPRESSIONS Track 075

Listen and match each question with its correct answer.

1. Do you know your neighbors?
2. What do you like about living in the suburbs?
3. Do you have any problems with your neighbors?
4. Have you met your new neighbor yet?
5. Do you ever get together with your neighbors?

WARM-UP Track 076

Listen and check what the speaker likes to do.

1. In summer, I like to sit on my porch and wave to my neighbors.
2. I love to plant flowers in my yard, but I hate to mow the lawn.
3. I volunteer at my local fire station, where I cook meals for the firefighters.
4. There's nothing better than having a barbecue and inviting my friends and neighbors.
5. I organize a lot of community events. It makes me happy to bring people together.

LISTEN FOR IT Track 077

Listen and check the correct description of the speaker's neighbors.

1. My neighbor is so noisy at night. I can't sleep well.
2. My neighbors invite me to a barbecue at their house every summer.
3. A family of four moved into the apartment next to mine yesterday.
4. I live next door to my aunt, so I get to see my cousins almost every day.
5. I live next to a fire station, so it can be very loud at times.

TRUE OR FALSE Track 078

Listen and write T for true or F for false.

1. **W** I'm having a small group of people over tomorrow night for dinner. My sister and her husband are coming over with their son. Also joining us is my neighbor who just moved in. He and my husband play golf together on weekends.
2. **M** I have some very interesting neighbors. Henry, who lives upstairs from me, is a writer. I hear him typing on his computer. Downstairs, in apartment 102, is a woman who works as a model. Edward, who lives down the hall, is a nice man. But he plays his music too loudly, so I sometimes have to ask him to be quiet.
3. **W** In my neighborhood, I organized a neighborhood association. I get together with other residents to discuss problems. We work out ways to improve our community. We managed to stop a thief who was stealing flower pots from front yards. It's good to take care of our community together.

LISTENING PRACTICE Track 079

Listen and choose the correct answer.

Questions 1 and 2 refer to the following dialog.

W Do you and your wife ever get together with your neighbors?

M We see each other socially about once a month. They often have us over for dinner.

W That' s nice. Do their children get along with your daughter?

M Oh, yes. They have a daughter who's the same age as our Becky. They are in the same class at school.

Questions 3 and 4 refer to the following dialog.

W How do you like your new apartment, Steve?

M It's fine. I've finally met some of my neighbors.

W What are they like?

M The neighbors down the hall are quiet and friendly. The family upstairs are nice too, but noisy. It's a couple with two small children. One child likes to run and play a lot. The other is always jumping rope. Sometimes they start at 6:00 a.m.

W Well, that's natural. They're just kids.

Questions 5 and 6 refer to the following talk.

M There are many things I like about my neighborhood. I have been a resident of this area for about 3 years. The people are all very friendly, and there is a good community spirit. Everyone in my street is very considerate. When I was very sick a year ago, four of my neighbors took turns to bring me food. That's why I like living in the suburbs. When I lived in the city, I didn't know any of my neighbors.

DICTATION 1 Track 080

A. Listen and fill in the blanks.

1. My neighbor is so noisy at night. I can't sleep well.
2. My neighbors invite me to a barbecue at their house every summer.
3. A family of four moved into the apartment next to mine yesterday.
4. I live next door to my aunt, so I get to see my cousins almost every day.
5. I live next to a fire station, so it can be very loud at times.

B. Listen and fill in the blanks.

W Do you and your wife ever get together with your neighbors?

M We see each other socially about once a month. They often have us over for dinner.

W That' s nice. Do their children get along with your daughter?

M Oh, yes. They have a daughter who's the same age as our Becky. They are in the same class at school.

C. Listen and fill in the blanks.

W How do you like your new apartment, Steve?

M It's fine. I've finally met some of my neighbors.

W What are they like?

M The neighbors down the hall are quiet and friendly. The family upstairs are nice too, but noisy. It's a couple with two small children. One child likes to run and play a lot. The other is always jumping rope. Sometimes they start at 6:00 a.m.

W Well, that's natural. They're just kids.

LISTENING TEST Track 081

Listen and choose the correct answer.

Questions 1 and 2 refer to the following dialog.

M Have your new neighbors moved in yet?
W Yes. They're nice, but there's already a problem.
M Are they noisy?
W It's a big family. They have four children, but they're surprisingly quiet. The problem is their dog.
M Oh, does it keep you awake at night?
W No, but it gets me up too early with its barking.
M Hmm, you might have to get used to getting up early.

Questions 3 and 4 refer to the following dialog.

W What do you like about living in the suburbs, Dave?
M There are so many good things. My kids can play on the lawn in the front yard while I sit on the porch and relax. I see my neighbors all the time, and everyone waves or stops to chat when I'm sitting outside.
W Is there anything negative about the suburbs?
M Not for me. I work at the local fire station and it's only a ten-minute walk from my house.
W Lucky you. I have to drive for an hour to get to work at the hospital.
M Yeah, I think I'm pretty lucky, and my kids live near their school, so it's good for all of us.

Questions 5 and 6 refer to the following dialog.

M I hear you're having a party, Lisa.
W Yes, it's my brother's birthday, and I want to have some people over for a small celebration.
M Will it be family only?
W No, we're really good friends with our neighbors so they'll be coming too. It's going to be potluck, so everyone will bring some food or drink to share.
M That's a good idea. It will make things much easier for you.
W Yes, and some of my neighbors are really good cooks. Hey, why don't you come? My brother really likes you.
M I'd love to. What should I bring?
W How about some kind of dessert?

DICTATION 2 Track 082

A. Listen and fill in the blanks.

M Have your new neighbors moved in yet?
W Yes. They're nice but there's already a problem.
M Are they noisy?
W It's a big family. They have four children, but they're surprisingly quiet. The problem is their dog.
M Oh, does it keep you awake at night?
W No, but it gets me up too early with its barking.
M Hmm, you might have to get used to getting up early.

B. Listen and fill in the blanks.

W What do you like about living in the suburbs, Dave?
M There are so many good things. My kids can play on the lawn in the front yard while I sit on the porch and relax. I see my neighbors all the time, and everyone waves or stops to chat when I'm sitting outside.
W Is there anything negative about the suburbs?
M Not for me. I work at the local fire station and it's only a ten-minute walk from my house.
W Lucky you. I have to drive for an hour to get to work at the hospital.
M Yeah, I think I'm pretty lucky, and my kids live near their school, so it's good for all of us.

C. Listen and fill in the blanks.

M I hear you're having a party, Lisa.
W Yes, it's my brother's birthday, and I want to have some people over for a small celebration.
M Will it be family only?
W No, we're really good friends with our neighbors so they'll be coming too. It's going to be potluck, so everyone will bring some food or drink to share.
M That's a good idea. It will make things much easier for you.
W Yes, and some of my neighbors are really good cooks. Hey, why don't you come? My brother really likes you.
M I'd love to. What should I bring?
W How about some kind of dessert?

Unit 10 The Weather Forecast

KEY WORDS Track 083

Listen for these words and phrases.

sunny	overcast
humid	chilly
snow	hail

drizzle | chance
lightning | heat wave

KEY EXPRESSIONS Track 084

Listen and match each question with its correct answer.

1. What's summer like in Seoul?
2. What's it like outside?
3. How was the weather in New York last spring?
4. Is it always this hot?
5. Is it supposed to rain a lot next week?

WARM-UP Track 085

Listen and check what kind of weather the speaker is discussing.

1. Even in the spring it snows between 5-7 centimeters.
2. Look at that flash! You'll hear thunder any moment now.
3. I should water our yard. Everything is dying in this heat wave.
4. The clouds are so low and heavy today.
5. There's not a cloud in the sky today!

LISTEN FOR IT Track 086

Listen and check what the weather was like yesterday.

1. Did you see the hail yesterday? It was as big as a baseball!
2. I had to take an umbrella. It was only drizzling, but I would have gotten very wet.
3. I visited Boston yesterday, but it was much colder than I had expected.
4. The thunder was so loud yesterday. My cat hid under my bed!
5. It was so hot yesterday—much hotter than it usually is in May.

TRUE OR FALSE Track 087

Listen and write T for true or F for false.

1. **W** Get yourself an umbrella for just $9.95. They come in all colors and are large enough so you won't need your raincoat. They can even keep the sun off your face on those bright sunny days. It looks like rain, so why wait?
2. **M** How was your vacation to Hawaii, Gail?
   W Great. It only rained one day. The sun was out the rest of the time.
   M Was it hot?
   W It was warm, but it got a little cool during the rain.
   M Sounds wonderful.
3. **W** What's it like outside?
   M It's pouring rain.
   W I'm tired of this wet weather.
   M I know. But the forecast said it should be dry tomorrow with a very small chance of rain.

LISTENING PRACTICE Track 088

Listen and choose the correct answer.

Questions 1 and 2 refer to the following dialog.

W I'm fed up with this weather.
M Why? I thought you liked the rain.
W Not this much! And I'm off work next week. Is it supposed to rain a lot next week?
M No, it's going to be fairly dry.
W Good. Maybe I'll be able to go hiking during my week off. I really don't want to spend my holiday sitting at home watching TV.
M You know, it is possible to go hiking in the rain.
W Yeah, I guess so. But it's more fun when it's sunny.

Questions 3 and 4 refer to the following dialog.

M Is it always this hot? I'm dying of heat.
W No, we're having a heat wave. It's usually around 35°C, but this week it's 40°.
M I don't know how you can live here! I'm glad I'm only visiting.
W You get used to the heat when you live here. I mean, when I visit you in Canada in the summer, I feel kind of cold. When you are wearing shorts and a T-shirt, I always need a sweater.
M Oh, that's true. You always ask me to turn off the air conditioning when you visit me.

Questions 5 and 6 refer to the following dialog.

M How was your business trip to Korea? You were there for a long time.
M Yes, I was there from April through September. It was great. I was setting up a new branch of our company.
W What's summer like in Seoul?
M It's really hot and humid. But there was plenty of air conditioning everywhere that I went.
W That's good. I really don't like humid weather.
M I know what you mean. I sweated a lot whenever I had to go outside.

W That's tough when you are wearing a business suit.

M Yes, but I bought some great light suits while I was there. That helped.

DICTATION 1 Track 089

A. Listen and fill in the blanks.

1. Did you see the hail yesterday? It was as big as a baseball!
2. I had to take an umbrella. It was only drizzling, but I would have gotten very wet.
3. I visited Boston yesterday, but it was much colder than I had expected.
4. The thunder was so loud yesterday. My cat hid under my bed!
5. It was so hot yesterday—much hotter than it usually is in May.

B. Listen and fill in the blanks.

W I'm fed up with this weather.

M Why? I thought you liked the rain.

W Not this much! And I'm off work next week. Is it supposed to rain a lot next week?

M No, it's going to be fairly dry.

W Good. Maybe I'll be able to go hiking during my week off. I really don't want to spend my holiday sitting at home watching TV.

M You know, it is possible to go hiking in the rain.

W Yeah, I guess so. But it's more fun when it's sunny.

C. Listen and fill in the blanks.

M Is it always this hot? I'm dying of heat.

W No, we're having a heat wave. It's usually around 35°C, but this week it's 40°.

M I don't know how you can live here! I'm glad I'm only visiting.

W You get used to the heat when you live here. I mean, when I visit you in Canada in the summer, I feel kind of cold. When you are wearing shorts and a T-shirt, I always need a sweater.

M Oh, that's true. You always ask me to turn off the air conditioning when you visit me.

LISTENING TEST Track 090

Listen and choose the correct answer.

Questions 1 and 2 refer to the following dialog.

W The sky is getting darker and darker.

M Yes, and it's getting cold. I think a storm is coming.

W Is it supposed to rain a lot today?

M Yes, and there may be some thunder and lightning.

W We'd better get inside before it starts pouring rain.

M Good idea. And you know how scared I am of lightning.

W Yes, I remember that time we were on the golf course during a storm. You looked so scared! But the sky was so beautiful.

Questions 3 and 4 refer to the following dialog.

M What's the weather forecast for this weekend?

W The weather lady said it should be warmer, but there's a chance of rain.

M Do you know what the temperature might be?

W She said we can expect lows in the mid-50s and highs in the low 60s.

M That doesn't sound too bad. It's much better than the hail we had yesterday.

Questions 5 and 6 refer to the following dialog.

W I'm thinking of visiting New York. You've been there, haven't you, Tom?

M Yes, I went there last spring.

W How was the weather in New York last spring? Is that a good time to go?

M It was sunny, but the mornings and nights were a little cold. The afternoons were nice. I was there in March, but I think April would be better. Spring is definitely better than winter for a trip. The city can get a lot of snow in winter, and the summers get really hot.

W OK, I'll book a flight for April. I've always wanted to go there.

DICTATION 2 Track 091

A. Listen and fill in the blanks.

W The sky is getting darker and darker.

M Yes, and it's getting cold. I think a storm is coming.

W Is it supposed to rain a lot today?

M Yes, and there may be some thunder and lightning.

W We'd better get inside before it starts pouring rain.

M Good idea. And you know how scared I am of lightning.

W Yes, I remember that time we were on the golf

course during a storm. You looked so scared! But the sky was so beautiful.

B. Listen and fill in the blanks.

M What's the weather forecast for this weekend?
W The weather lady said it should be warmer, but there's a chance of rain.
M Do you know what the temperature might be?
W She said we can expect lows in the mid-50s and highs in the low 60s.
M That doesn't sound too bad. It's much better than the hail we had yesterday.

C. Listen and fill in the blanks.

W I'm thinking of visiting New York. You've been there, haven't you, Tom?
M Yes, I went there last spring.
W How was the weather in New York last spring? Is that a good time to go?
M It was sunny, but the mornings and nights were a little cold. The afternoons were nice. I was there in March, but I think April would be better. Spring is definitely better than winter for a trip. The city can get a lot of snow in winter, and the summers get really hot.
W OK, I'll book a flight for April. I've always wanted to go there.

Unit 11 My Day

KEY WORDS Track 092

Listen for these words and phrases.

do the laundry	vacuum
seldom	charge (a phone)
work out	make the bed
pick up (the kids)	buy groceries
take out the trash	shave

KEY EXPRESSIONS Track 093

Listen and match each question with its correct answer.

1. Do you do any exercise?
2. Who does the laundry in your household?
3. How often do you vacuum your room?
4. Did you take the trash out?
5. Can I borrow your phone?

WARM-UP Track 094

Listen and check what the speaker does on a typical day.

1. I get up, take a shower, shave, and brush my teeth.
2. I pick up the kids from school at 3:30 every day.
3. I seldom make my bed in the morning; I do it every night.
4. I brush my teeth twice a day. Once in the morning, and once at night.
5. I buy groceries so that I can cook dinner.

LISTEN FOR IT Track 095

Listen and check what the speaker did.

1. I forgot to charge my cell phone last night. I couldn't reply to my girlfriend's texts, and now she is mad at me.
2. I vacuumed the whole house before work. But while I was out, my dog made a big mess.
3. I cut myself shaving, so I had to go to work with a band aid on my face.
4. I worked out at the gym this morning. I also took a fitness class from a new trainer. Now I'm so tired.
5. I wanted to wear my green shirt, so I washed it this morning. But my dryer stopped working, and I couldn't wear the shirt after all.

TRUE OR FALSE Track 096

Listen and write T for true or F for false.

1. M I always eat breakfast. I usually have eggs. Sometimes I also eat toast. But I never drink coffee. I drink lots of tea.
2. W I usually go to bed at 11:00. I read in bed for a while, or watch TV. I fall asleep around midnight. I sleep about seven hours a night.
3. M I do the laundry every day. I have three children, so there are a lot of dirty clothes. I always separate light and dark clothes.

LISTENING PRACTICE Track 097

Listen and choose the correct answer.

Questions 1 and 2 refer to the following dialog.

W Are you in the bathroom, dear?
M Yes, I am. I'm shaving. And then I need to brush my hair.
W Will you be much longer? I still need to put on my makeup.
M I'm almost done. Just give me a minute.
W OK, but please hurry. I don't want to be late.

M I know. Why don't you make the bed while you're waiting?

Questions 3 and 4 refer to the following dialog.

W Did you take out the trash, Mark?
M Sorry, Mom. I completely forgot about that. Can I do it tomorrow?
W No, you know that you are supposed to do it every day.
M But Mom, it's raining.
W Well, it wasn't raining earlier. You should have taken it out before it started to rain.
M This is so unfair.

Questions 5 and 6 refer to the following dialog.

M How often do you vacuum your house?
W Not as often as I should. Actually, my husband vacuums every other day. He also washes the dishes.
M Do your children help you with housework?
W They often do the laundry. I do the shopping, cook, and make the beds, so I expect them to do something.
M You sure have a helpful family!
W Yes, they are usually very good about helping.

DICTATION 1 Track 098

A. Listen and fill in the blanks.

1. I forgot to charge my cell phone last night. I couldn't reply to my girlfriend's texts, and now she is mad at me.
2. I vacuumed the whole house before work. But while I was out, my dog made a big mess.
3. I cut myself shaving, so I had to go to work with a band aid on my face.
4. I worked out at the gym this morning. I also took a fitness class from a new trainer. Now I'm so tired.
5. I wanted to wear my green shirt, so I washed it this morning. But my dryer stopped working, and I couldn't wear the shirt after all.

B. Listen and fill in the blanks.

W Are you in the bathroom, dear?
M Yes, I am. I'm shaving. And then I need to brush my hair.
W Will you be much longer? I still need to put on my makeup.
M I'm almost done. Just give me a minute.
W OK, but please hurry. I don't want to be late.
M I know. Why don't you make the bed while you're waiting.

C. Listen and fill in the blanks.

W Did you take out the trash, Mark?
M Sorry, Mom. I completely forgot about that. Can I do it tomorrow?
W No, you know that you are supposed to do it every day.
M But Mom, it's raining.
W Well, it wasn't raining earlier. You should have taken it out before it started to rain.
M This is so unfair.

LISTENING TEST Track 099

Listen and choose the correct answer.

Questions 1 and 2 refer to the following dialog.

M Do you do any exercise, Briana?
W Yes, I work out every other day: usually weight lifting. And I walk to school every day.
M Do you still play tennis?
W Not anymore, but I took up golf last year. I'm getting quite good. What about you, Chris? Are you into any sports?
M Not really. But I ride my bike a lot. I used to take the subway to work, but it took about 45 minutes. If I ride my bike, I can get to the restaurant in 30 minutes.
W That's convenient.

Questions 3 and 4 refer to the following dialog.

W What do you do every evening?
M I come home from school at 4:30. I usually do my homework until 6:30 and then I have dinner.
W Do you ever help your mother cook dinner?
M Yes, sometimes. But I can't make tasty food like my mom does. I always wash the dishes after dinner.
W That's nice of you. Who does the laundry in your household?
M My mom. She says I don't get the clothes clean enough.
W Same here. My mom washes all of my clothes.

Questions 5 and 6 refer to the following dialog.

M Can I borrow your phone, Jenny?
W Sure. Did you forget to charge yours again, Tom?
M Yeah. And I have to call my dad to let him know I'm about to leave.
W Do you call him every day?
M Yeah, he likes to know where I am.

W I seldom call my mom and dad. But I do send texts.

M I think most people send texts, but my dad always wants me to call him. He says texts are for lazy people.

W And I guess he likes to hear your voice.

M Maybe.

DICTATION 2 Track 100

A. Listen and fill in the blanks.

M Do you do any exercise, Briana?

W Yes, I work out every other day: usually weight lifting. And I walk to school every day.

M Do you still play tennis?

W Not anymore, but I took up golf last year. I'm getting quite good. What about you, Chris? Are you into any sports?

M Not really. But I ride my bike a lot. I used to take the subway to work, but it took about 45 minutes. If I ride my bike, I can get to the restaurant in 30 minutes.

W That's convenient.

B. Listen and fill in the blanks.

W What do you do every evening?

M I come home from school at 4:30. I usually do my homework until 6:30 and then I have dinner.

W Do you ever help your mother cook dinner?

M Yes, sometimes. But I can't make tasty food like my mom does. I always wash the dishes after dinner.

W That's nice of you. Who does the laundry in your household?

M My mom. She says I don't get the clothes clean enough.

W Same here. My mom washes all of my clothes.

C. Listen and fill in the blanks.

M Can I borrow your phone, Jenny?

W Sure. Did you forget to charge yours again, Tom?

M Yeah. And I have to call my dad to let him know I'm about to leave.

W Do you call him every day?

M Yeah, he likes to know where I am.

W I seldom call my mom and dad. But I do send texts.

M I think most people send texts, but my dad always wants me to call him. He says texts are for lazy people.

W And I guess he likes to hear your voice.

M Maybe.

Unit 12 Let's Talk

KEY WORDS Track 101

Listen for these words and phrases.

telecommute	local call
international call	call back
put in one's contacts	caller ID
expect	video conference
service	text message

KEY EXPRESSIONS Track 102

Listen and match each question with its correct answer.

1. When do you expect her to get back?
2. May I have the number for Tom Leeds in Denver, Colorado?
3. Can I speak to your mother?
4. What telephone network do you use?
5. How do I make an international call?

WARM-UP Track 103

Listen and check what the speaker wants to do.

1. My cell phone service is terrible. I need to change to a new provider.
2. Could you give me your new number? I'd like to add it to my contacts list.
3. I'm expecting an important call, so I need everyone to be very quiet when the phone rings.
4. I have to call my sister in Spain. Can you tell me the country code for Spain?
5. I'm going to organize a party for my parents' wedding anniversary. Do you know the number for the flower shop on 3rd Street?

LISTEN FOR IT Track 104

Listen and check why the speaker is calling.

1. **M** Hi, this is Brian Tanaka. I got your message, and I'm returning your call.
2. **W** Can I speak to Anita Walker at extension 302?
3. **M** Hi, Mary. It looks like you can't come to the phone. I just wanted to let you know that I won't be home for dinner.
4. **W** I'm calling about your advertisement on your website. Do you still have any of the pink cakes left?

5. **M** Hey, Amanda! Did you get my text? Call me back! I need to talk to you.

TRUE OR FALSE Track 105

Listen and write T for true or F for false.

1. **M** This message is for Bruce Miles. It's Gerry at Steven Wong's Dental Services. I'm calling to confirm your appointment for Wednesday May 23rd. Please give me a call to let me know if you are still able to make the appointment. Remember, we may charge you if you fail to attend an appointment without giving us at least 24-hour's notice.
2. **M** Hello.
   M Hi, Mrs. Evans. Is Marcy there?
   W May I ask who's calling?
   M It's her friend Bill.
   W Just a moment. I'll get her.
3. **W** Thank you for calling Midway Airlines. All our lines are busy at this time, but please hold and we will answer your call as soon as a representative is available. If you are calling to confirm or change your flight, please have your reservation number ready.

LISTENING PRACTICE Track 106

Listen and choose the correct answer.

Questions 1 and 2 refer to the following dialog.

W Directory Assistance.
M May I have the number for Tom Leeds in Denver, Colorado?
W Thank you. I'd like to check the name. Is the last name R-E-E-D?
M No, it's L-E-E-D-S.
W I see. Just a moment. The number is 515-739-0882. May I help you with anything else?
M No. That's all, thank you.
W Have a great day.

Questions 3 and 4 refer to the following dialog.

M Hey, Lisa. I want to call my old homestay family in Japan. How do I make an international call? I've never done it before.
W That's easy. Well, first you'll need to enter the country code.
M OK, let me just look that up… Got it. It's 82… No, it's 81 for Japan.
W So just dial the country code, then the area code. Then just call the phone number.
M That sounds easy.
W It is! Just let me know if you have any trouble getting through.

Questions 5 and 6 refer to the following dialog.

M Is Sandy there?
W I'm afraid not. She left about an hour ago.
M I see. It's Don from her math class. When do you expect her to get back?
W She went to a 7:30 movie, so she should be back about 10:00.
M I see. Could you tell her that Don called and I'll call her tomorrow?
W Sure, I'll tell her.

DICTATION 1 Track 107

A. Listen and fill in the blanks.

1. Hi, this is Brian Tanaka. I got your message, and I'm returning your call.
2. Can I speak to Anita Walker at extension 302?
3. Hi, Mary. It looks like you can't come to the phone. I just wanted to let you know that I won't be home for dinner.
4. I'm calling about your advertisement on your website. Do you still have any of the pink cakes left?
5. Hey, Amanda! Did you get my text? Call me back! I need to talk to you.

B. Listen and fill in the blanks.

W Directory Assistance.
M May I have the number for Tom Leeds in Denver, Colorado?
W Thank you. I'd like to check the name. Is the last name R-E-E-D?
M No, it's L-E-E-D-S.
W I see. Just a moment. The number is 515-739-0882. May I help you with anything else?
M No. That's all, thank you.
W Have a great day.

C. Listen and fill in the blanks.

M Hey, Lisa. I want to call my old homestay family in Japan. How do I make an international call? I've never done it before.
W That's easy. Well, first you'll need to enter the country code.
M OK, let me just look that up… Got it. It's 82… No, it's 81 for Japan.
W So just dial the country code, then the area code. Then just call the phone number.
M That sounds easy.

W It is! Just let me know if you have any trouble getting through.

LISTENING TEST Track 108

Listen and choose the correct answer.

Questions 1 and 2 refer to the following dialog.

M Hello?

W1 Hello. Is that Kevin? This is Helen Green. Can I speak to your mother?

M Yes. Let me pass the phone to her… Mom! It's for you!

W2 Hello?

W1 Hi, Lisa. It's Helen. Are you free tomorrow? I have the day off work, and I thought it might be nice to meet for lunch.

W2 Definitely. Do you want to go to that new place on Broadway?

W1 You read my mind! Why don't I pick you up at 11:30?

W2 I'll be ready!

Questions 3 and 4 refer to the following dialog.

W I'm trying to make a call, but I can't get a good signal.

M Really? I'm not having any trouble. You have the same kind of phone as me.

W The problem is not the phone. It's the network. I get really bad service. I even have to pay extra for caller ID. I hate it. What phone company do you use?

M Mobile Com. They have the best coverage.

W Hmm, I've seen their advertisements. They have that really annoying man promoting the service.

M He might be annoying, but the service is good. You should switch.

Questions 5 and 6 refer to the following dialog.

M How's your new job going, You Jung?

W It's great. I love it. I telecommute three days a week, so it's very convenient.

M Isn't it difficult to have meetings? I mean, you don't spend much time in the office.

W Oh, that's not a problem at all. We use various computer programs, and we do a lot of video conferences.

M Of course. But don't you find it difficult to concentrate when you are not in the same room as your co-workers?

W Not really. And the meetings are usually much shorter than when we meet at the office.

DICTATION 2 Track 109

A. Listen and fill in the blanks.

M Hello?

W1 Hello. Is that Kevin? This is Helen Green. Can I speak to your mother?

M Yes. Let me pass the phone to her… Mom! It's for you!

W2 Hello?

W1 Hi Lisa. It's Helen. Are you free tomorrow? I have the day off work, and I thought it might be nice to meet for lunch.

W2 Definitely. Do you want to go to that new place on Broadway?

W1 You read my mind! Why don't I pick you up at 11:30?

W2 I'll be ready!

B. Listen and fill in the blanks.

W I'm trying to make a call, but I can't get a good signal.

M Really? I'm not having any trouble. You have the same kind of phone as me.

W The problem is not the phone. It's the network. I get really bad service. I even have to pay extra for caller ID. I hate it. What phone company do you use?

M Mobile Com. They have the best coverage.

W Hmm, I've seen their advertisements. They have that really annoying man promoting the service.

M He might be annoying, but the service is good. You should switch.

C. Listen and fill in the blanks.

M How's your new job going, You Jung?

W It's great. I love it. I telecommute three days a week, so it's very convenient.

M Isn't it difficult to have meetings? I mean, you don't spend much time in the office.

W Oh, that's not a problem at all. We use various computer programs, and we do a lot of video conferences.

M Of course. But don't you find it difficult to concentrate when you are not in the same room as your co-workers?

W Not really. And the meetings are usually much shorter than when we meet at the office.

How to Use the App

1. Scan the QR code at the back of the book.

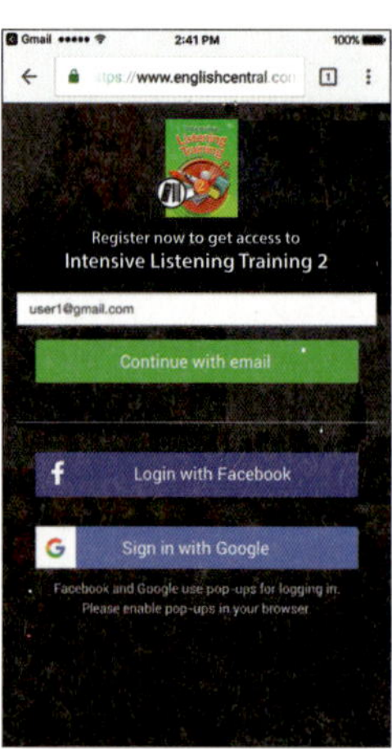

2. Type your email address. Then click on "Continue with email."

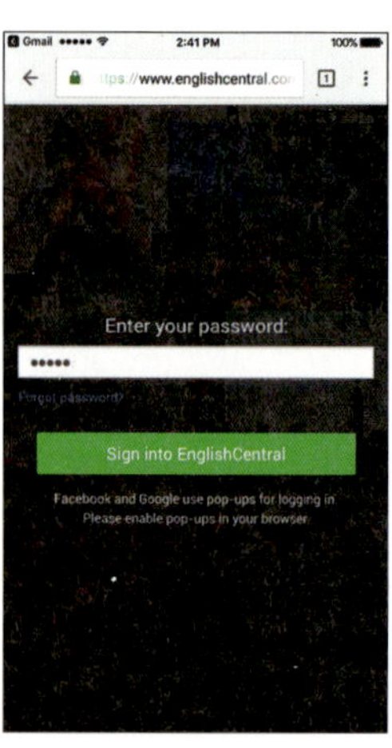

3a. If you already have an EnglishCentral account, enter your password.

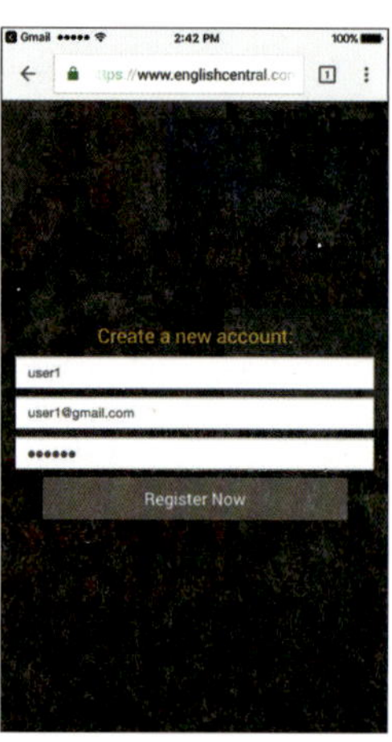

3b. If you don't have an EnglishCentral account, add your name, email, and password. Then click on "Register Now."

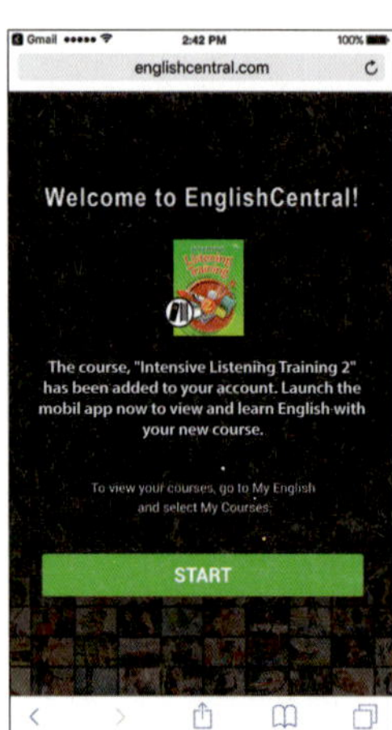

4. You now have the textbook course in your account. Click on "START."

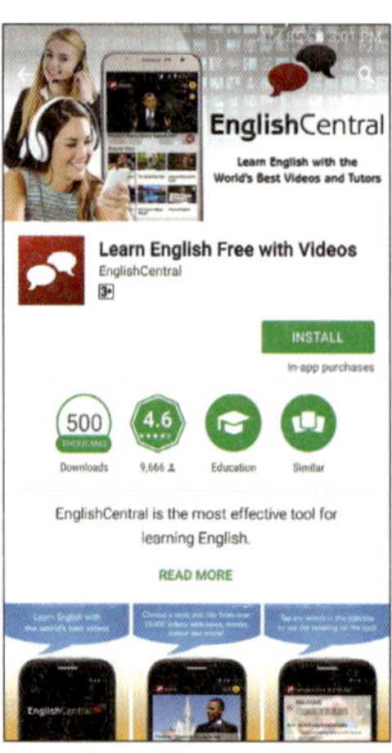

5. Install the EnglishCentral app.

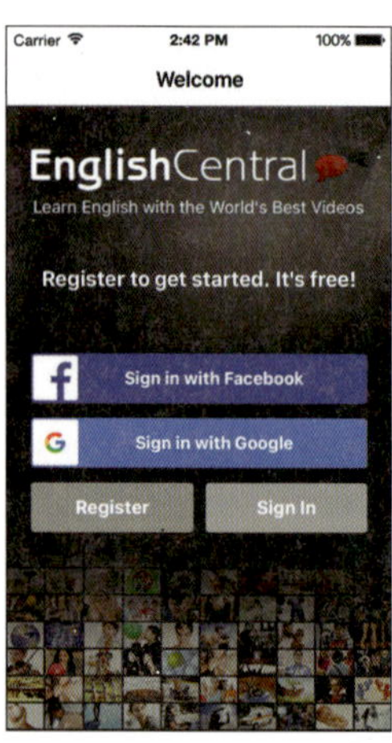

6. Click on "Sign In." Sign in with the email address that you used in #2.

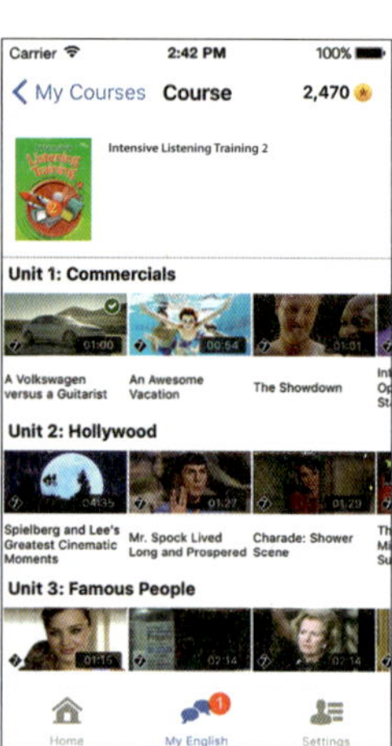

7. You will see your textbook course when you log in. Complete all the units to finish the course.

Intensive Listening Training

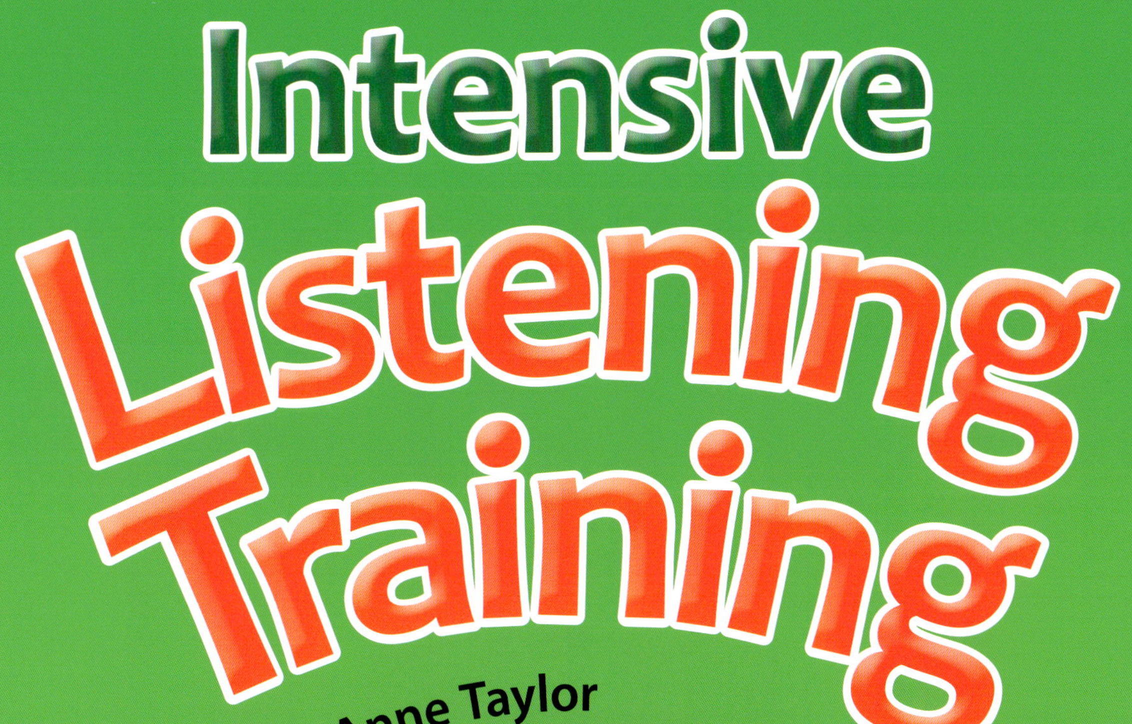

David Bohlke • Anne Taylor

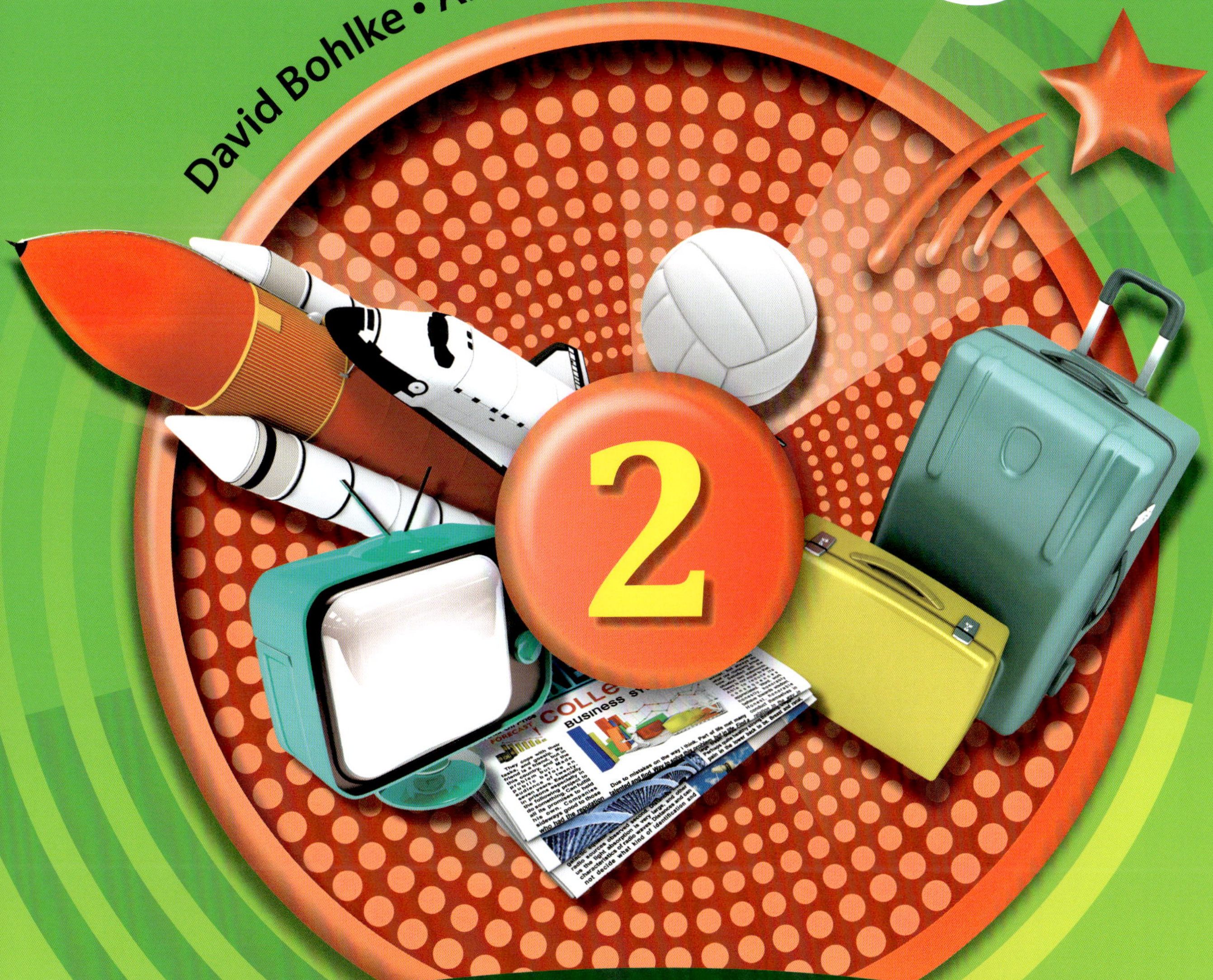

2

Answer Key

Intensive Listening Training

2

David Bohlke • Anne Taylor

Answer Key

Unit 1 Tell Me About Yourself

KEY EXPRESSIONS

1. (A) 2. (E) 3. (D) 4. (C) 5. (B)

WARM-UP

1. (A) 2. (B) 3. (A) 4. (B) 5. (A)

LISTEN FOR IT

1. (A) 2. (B) 3. (A) 4.(A) 5. (A)

TRUE OR FALSE

1. (A) F (B) F
2. (A) T (B) T
3. (A) T (B) F

LISTENING PRACTICE

1. (B) 2. (C) 3. (D) 4. (C) 5. (B)
6. (D)

DICTATION 1

A.

1. I met my wife when we were both students. We've been married for ten years. Her name is Lisa.
2. My father is a very interesting man. He likes to golf, travel, and spend time with his children. His favorite hobby is probably taking pictures.
3. I have too many numbers to remember! My telephone number, my apartment number, my social security number. But the most important is my PIN at the bank.
4. My parents are originally from Florida, but they moved to California 13 years ago. We live on Market Street in San Francisco. Our apartment number is 302a.
5. My name is Beth. I was born in France on May 25, 1995. We moved to the United States when I was five years old.

B.

M Your résumé looks great, Ms. Parker. We just have one more question for you.
W Thank you.
M I see you were born in Spain. Do you speak Spanish?
W Yes. I speak both English and Spanish fluently.
M Wonderful. We have a lot of customers who are Spanish speakers. We'll call you in the next couple of days with our decision.

C.

M Hello. Are you Mrs. Lynne?
W Actually, Lynne is my first name. My family name is Webster. My husband is Ted Webster. He works in your office.
M Oh, of course. I'm sorry. I'm Kelly Madison.
W How do you do, Mr. Madison?
M How do you do? It's nice to meet you.

LISTENING TEST

1. (C) 2. (A) 3. (D) 4. (A) 5. (D)
6. (A)

DICTATION 2

A.

M Excuse me. Could you help me a moment with this form?
W Sure.
M What does DOB mean?
W It means date of birth.
M Oh. And how about gender?
W That means, "Are you a man or a woman?" Just check 'M'.
M Thank you. I appreciate your help.
W It was my pleasure.

B.

M OK. That completes your purchase. Do you want to take the table with you, or have it delivered?
W I'd like it delivered, please. How much will that cost?
M Delivery is free.
W Wonderful. I'd like it delivered to 3420 Golden State Drive, Anyville, California. And the zip code is 59302.
M Could you also give me a phone number?
W 665-4456.

C.

M I'm afraid some information is missing from your visa application. Do you have your ID card with you?
M Yes, here it is.
W Oh, you were born in England?
M That's right. In Liverpool.
W Do you often go back to England?
M Not really. Most of my family live here in the US.
W Ah, I see.

Unit 2 Occupations

KEY EXPRESSIONS

1. (B) 2. (A) 3. (D) 4. (E) 5. (C)

WARM-UP

1. (B) 2. (A) 3. (B) 4. (B) 5. (A)

LISTEN FOR IT

1. (A) 2. (B) 3. (A) 4. (A) 5. (B)

TRUE OR FALSE

1. (A) T (B) F
2. (A) T (B) T
3. (A) F (B) F

LISTENING PRACTICE

1. (B) 2. (D) 3. (A) 4. (D) 5. (B)
6. (D)

DICTATION 1

A.

1. I'm sorry, but you need to fasten your seat belt. The plane will be landing soon.
2. I just need to take your temperature and I'll get your pills.
3. OK, here is $20, $40, $60, $80, $100. Is there anything else I can do for you today?
4. I have the fish for you, sir. And who ordered the spaghetti?
5. Please show me your driver's license. You were speeding, sir.

B.

I'm a university student and will graduate in a few months. I need to decide what I want to do after I graduate. My father is a doctor, and he wants me to be a doctor, too. But that would mean a lot more studying, and I don't think my grades are good enough. My mother is a teacher. She says I should do whatever I want to do. I'm interested in design and photography, so it might be fun to be a graphic designer. I'll travel for a few months, and then I will decide.

C.

I did something that many people find strange. I was an architect for many years. It was a good job. The pay was high, but the hours were so long. So I quit about five years ago. I wanted to have my own business and be my own boss. I studied for a certificate in hair styling and opened a salon in my home. I have a lot of customers, and I can stay home. I love it, but people think I'm a little crazy.

LISTENING TEST

1. (B) 2. (D) 3. (D) 4. (A) 5. (D)
6. (B)

DICTATION 2

A.

W How are you enjoying your new job?
M It's going well so far.
W What do you do on an average day?
M Well, first, I meet the pilot and the other flight attendants. Then, we do safety checks.
W What happens after that?
M That's when it gets very busy! The passengers start to board, and I have to help them find their seats. And once we start to fly, it's even busier while I hand out food and drinks.

B.

W How's life, Kenny? Are you taking your lunch break?
M Didn't you hear? I lost my job.
W Your teller job at the bank?
M Yes. I'm unemployed at the moment.
W I'm sorry to hear that.
M Not at all. I want to get into writing. Now I have the time.
W Are you going to get a website?
M Yes, and things look promising.
W Well, good luck, Kenny.

C.

M I heard that you retired.
W Yes, after twenty years as a mechanic.
M Do you miss work at all?
W Sure, sometimes. But now I can work on my own car!
M That's true. Are you going to take up any hobbies?
W Actually, I'm going to start teaching a class on car repair at the community center once a month.
M Nice.

Unit 3 Describing Things

KEY EXPRESSIONS

1. (C) 2. (D) 3. (A) 4. (E) 5. (B)

WARM-UP

1. (A) 2. (B) 3. (A) 4. (A) 5. (A)

LISTEN FOR IT

1. (B) 2. (A) 3. (A) 4. (B) 5. (A)

TRUE OR FALSE

1. (A) F (B) T
2. (A) T (B) T
3. (A) T (B) T

LISTENING PRACTICE

1. (C) 2. (C) 3. (C) 4. (B) 5. (D)
6. (C)

DICTATION 1

A.

1. It's long, and I wear it around my neck. I wear a thick one made of wool in the winter.
2. These are long and thin, and can be made of wood, plastic, or metal. They are used for eating.
3. We use these round metal objects to buy things, but they don't usually have a high value.
4. It's usually square or rectangular and is made of glass. Every house has many so that the light can come in.
5. It's soft and comfortable to sit on while you watch TV or read a book.

B.

I had a quiet weekend. On Saturday, I was busy all day. I cleaned my house and washed all my dirty clothes. On Sunday, I painted my bedroom. It used to have brown walls. But brown is a sad color. So I painted it light green. Now it looks so clean and fresh. Green is a relaxing color, so I think I will sleep better now.

C.

W Oh, no. I've wrapped all the presents. But I forgot to put labels on them.
M Well, maybe we can work out what everything is. How about this large square box?
W Um, I put Julie's sweater in a square box. How heavy is it?
M It's not at all heavy.
W OK, that's Julie's gift. Can you find a very hard box? Like something made of wood?
M This feels like wood.
W Great, that's a wooden box for Grandpa.
M This is easy. Let's keep going.

LISTENING TEST

1. (B) 2. (C) 3. (D) 4. (A) 5. (B)
6. (D)

DICTATION 2

A.

M How was your weekend, Jill?
W Great. I went to my sister's wedding.
M Oh yeah? How was it?
W It was small and private, but very pretty. My sister was so happy.
M How was her dress?
W It was nice. It wasn't traditional. It was light yellow and short, but very pretty.

B.

W I left my glasses in here after my math class last week. Have you seen them?
M I found three pairs last week. And two pencil cases and a water bottle. Can you describe your glasses for me?
W Well, they are metal. Actually, they are red metal, with a silver line along the side. Do you have them?
M I have a pair of blue metal glasses and a pair of red plastic glasses, but nothing that looks like yours.
W Oh, no. New glasses will be so expensive.
M I'm sorry. I just don't have them.

C.

W Larry asked me to take a tie to his office. He spilled coffee on himself.
M How about this blue one? Or this purple-and-gray one is nice.
W No. He told me which tie he wants, but I can't find it.
M What does it look like? I'll help you look.
W It is yellow with red spots.
M He wants that tie? It's so ugly.

W I agree, but Larry likes it. He says it makes his eyes look green.

Unit 4 Describing People

KEY EXPRESSIONS

1. (E) 2. (A) 3. (D) 4. (C) 5. (B)

WARM-UP

1. (B) 2. (A) 3. (A) 4. (B) 5. (A)

LISTEN FOR IT

1. (A) 2. (B) 3. (A) 4. (B) 5. (A)

TRUE OR FALSE

1. (A) F (B) F
2. (A) T (B) F
3. (A) T (B) T

LISTENING PRACTICE

1. (A) 2. (D) 3. (D) 4. (A) 5. (D)
6. (B)

DICTATION 1

A.

1. I cut my knee badly when I was ten, and you can still see where the injury was.
2. I'm losing all my hair, just like my father and grandfather did.
3. The hair on my chin is starting to get very long now.
4. My brother Ken is good-looking and wants to be a model.
5. My hair is full of bends and twists. It's hard to brush sometimes.

B.

Who was my favorite teacher in high school? That would be Mr. Madison, my math teacher. He was young—in his thirties, I suppose. He made math fun, you know. He was funny, always making us laugh. And he had really crazy hair. But he was really serious about his teaching and our learning. He helped us a lot after class when we needed it.

C.

Attention, shoppers. We have a lost child in the store. Please be on the lookout for a boy, aged four. His name is Sam, and he is wearing a red baseball cap and a green T-shirt. His hair is black and straight. He was last seen in the toy department. If you see this boy, please contact a clerk immediately.

LISTENING TEST

1. (A) 2. (D) 3. (C) 4. (A) 5. (D)
6. (D)

DICTATION 2

A.

W You don't have a girlfriend, do you, Joe?
M Me? No. Why?
W Do you want me to introduce you to my cousin Patty?
M I don't know. I'm not looking for a girlfriend.
W Well, she is pretty. She has short black hair, blue eyes, and she is very tall.
M I don't care about that. What is she like?
W She is very sweet. She is smart, too, but kind of serious.
M OK. When can I meet her?

B.

W I didn't know you had a large scar on your leg.
M This? Oh, yeah. I've had it for years.
W How did you get that scar?
M I fell off my bike. And I landed on a sharp stick.
W That's all? I thought it would be something like a shark bite. I mean—you surf a lot.
M Hey, I'm sorry if it's not an exciting story. It really hurt, you know!

C.

M How was your date, Cindy?
W Great. Ben is so cute.
M You like him then?
W Oh, yes. He is tall, handsome, and has beautiful brown eyes.
M What did you talk about?
W He's very interesting. He can draw and paint, too, so he's really artistic.

Unit 5 Finding Places

KEY EXPRESSIONS

1. (B) 2. (E) 3. (D) 4. (C) 5. (A)

WARM-UP

1. (A) 2. (B) 3. (B) 4. (B) 5. (A)

LISTEN FOR IT

1. (B) 2. (A) 3. (A) 4. (B) 5. (A)

TRUE OR FALSE

1. (A) T (B) F
2. (A) T (B) F
3. (A) F (B) T

LISTENING PRACTICE

1. (B) 2. (B) 3. (C) 4. (B) 5. (B)
6. (B)

DICTATION 1

A.

1. Turn right at the first traffic light.
2. Go east for three blocks.
3. Walk until you come to the third street.
4. Take a left after you pass the library.
5. Go up Lake Avenue until you see a church.

B.

I'll give you directions to get to my house. Listen carefully, or write them down. The address is 1680 Lincoln Way. Got that? 1680 Lincoln Way. Take Second Avenue—it's the fastest route. Go straight until you come to the intersection of Second Avenue and Henderson Street. There, take a left, go straight for another six blocks, and you'll come to Lincoln Way. Turn right, and look for a blue house.

C.

John, this is Cameron. Text me when you get this message. There's a party tomorrow at Mark and Edward's place. Do you know where they live? It's on Lexington Avenue. From your place, go east on Lexington until you come to Jameson Foods. They live behind there. Park your car at the store, and look for a white apartment building with blue stripes. They live in apartment 6B. Hope to see you around 7.

LISTENING TEST

1. (B) 2. (D) 3. (D) 4. (B) 5. (B)
6. (A)

DICTATION 2

A.

W Excuse me. Is there a bookstore around here?
M Yes, there's one on Davis Street.
W And where is that?
M Oh, go up this street. This is Mayfair Lane. Take it up to the traffic light.
W Yes . . .
M Take a right, and go one block. That's Davis.
W OK . . .
M You'll see a large sporting goods store. The bookstore's above that.
W Thank you very much.

B.

M Excuse me, but is this the way to the police station?
W No. It's not in this area.
M Isn't this Second Avenue?
W Sorry, this is Second Street.
M Oh, no. Where is Second Avenue?
W It's about eight blocks south of here.
M I see. Thanks.

C.

W Hello.
M Hey, Mary! It's Andrew. I can't find your apartment.
W Where are you now?
M I'm at the corner of McGregor and Park.
W You're close. Just walk east for a few minutes. You'll see a men's clothing store on the corner. Keep going straight, and cross the crosswalk. I'm the first door on the left.
M Got it. See you soon.

Unit 6 Making Plans

KEY EXPRESSIONS

1. (B) 2. (A) 3. (C) 4. (E) 5. (D)

WARM-UP

1. (A) 2. (B) 3. (B) 4. (B) 5. (A)

LISTEN FOR IT

1. (B) 2. (A) 3. (B) 4. (B) 5. (A)

TRUE OR FALSE

1. (A) T (B) F
2. (A) T (B) F
3. (A) T (B) T

LISTENING PRACTICE

1. (B) 2. (C) 3. (C) 4. (D) 5. (C)
6. (B)

DICTATION 1

A.

1. Angela, Susan wants you to call her right away.
2. Waiter, may we see the dessert menu?
3. Look, Bob. You got a warning letter from the gas company. You have to pay the bill immediately.
4. Get your money ready. Here comes the bus.
5. I like this jacket. Do you think it will fit me?

B.

People ask me what I want to do in the future. That's a difficult question to answer. I'll graduate next year, when I'm 22, so I need to make some decisions. I won't go to graduate school next year. But I will go eventually. I know that for sure. I want to get a job in the computer industry. I'll definitely get married someday, but I don't know when. It's possible that I will have children. But I'm not sure. I like kids, but want to have a career. I'll decide that with my husband.

C.

Excuse me, Doctor Lynne? Could we go over your schedule for today? As you know, I will be leaving a little early today. You have four appointments with patients this morning, from 10 to 12:30. At 12:30, Dr. Carrington will be stopping by to discuss some things. You have a meeting at 1:00, and that should last for about half an hour. For the rest of the day, you can see you will be pretty free. I'll be here until 3:30 to answer any calls.

LISTENING TEST

1. (C) 2. (B) 3. (A) 4. (D) 5. (C)
6. (B)

DICTATION 2

A.

M What are your summer plans, Megan?
W Well, I'm going to summer school in July and then going to Dallas.
M Dallas? Why are you going there?
W My friend is getting married on August 5th, so I'll attend her wedding.
M And after that?
W I'll visit my parents for a week and then return home.
M That sounds like a good summer.

B.

M Do you want to get together on Friday?
W What time?
M I'm meeting Greg at 5:00. Join us then.
W I can't. I have to work till 6:00.
M Meet us later for dinner then.
W OK. How about 7:30?
M Sounds good. Come to the Vega Café.
W I'll be there.

C.

Sometimes I feel very worried about the future. Humans do so many things that harm the Earth. My friends drive everywhere. I'm trying to persuade them to walk, ride bicycles, or use public transportation. I predict that if we all stop using cars at least one day a week, the air will be much less polluted. Why don't you try?

Unit 7 In the Past

KEY EXPRESSIONS

1. (B) 2. (C) 3. (A) 4. (E) 5. (D)

WARM-UP

1. (B) 2. (B) 3. (A) 4. (B) 5. (A)

LISTEN FOR IT

1. (B) 2. (A) 3. (B) 4. (A) 5. (B)

TRUE OR FALSE

1. (A) T (B) F
2. (A) T (B) T
3. (A) T (B) T

LISTENING PRACTICE

1. (D) 2. (C) 3. (C) 4. (C) 5. (D)
6. (B)

DICTATION 1

A.

1. Did you hear that, Roseanne? Can you get the door, please?
2. I left some room for a sweet treat. May we please see the dessert menu?
3. I feel so much cleaner now.
4. I'm glad we landed on time. But we need to go through Customs and Immigration now.
5. David, it was so nice of you. The sweater fits perfectly.

B.

Thank you for considering me for the job, sir. I graduated from university in 2010 with a degree in finance. I started work the same year as a manager for Wilson Jewelers. I worked there for 2 years, and then I returned to graduate school. I got my master's degree in business administration in 2014. Since then, I have been working as the China regional sales manager at Semtex Corporation. I have a proven record of sales, and I have established accounts worth over $34 million this year alone. My previous experience makes me ideal for this position.

C.

I had a good childhood. I am the youngest of four children. I have two older brothers and a sister. We often played together as kids. We used to play basketball, football, and go swimming every summer. It seems like I was never alone. Until I was 12, we lived in the countryside, but then my father got a new job so we moved to a city. Suddenly, we were living in an apartment on the 20th floor. None of us liked it very much.

LISTENING TEST

1. (D) 2. (C) 3. (A) 4. (C) 5. (B)
6. (A)

DICTATION 2

A.

W Hey, George. I tried to call and text you last night. Why didn't you answer?
M Sorry. I was feeling really sick last night so I turned off my phone and went to bed early.
W Are you OK now?
M I guess, but I still have a bit of a fever and my head really hurts.
W I'm sorry to hear that. Can I get anything for you?
M No, I'm just going to go home again after this meeting. I have to give a sales report. Then I'm going back to bed.

B.

M Welcome home. How was your trip?
W Great.
M Where did you go, again?
W We took a bus tour in Australia.
M That's right. Did you stay mostly in Sydney or did you travel around?
W We went all over. Like I said, it was a bus trip.
M How was the accommodation?
W We usually stayed in hotels, but sometimes we went camping or stayed in small private inns.

C.

M Happy birthday, Mom.
W Oh, Billy. Thank you. What a surprise!
M Look. I cooked you breakfast and Susan cleaned up the kitchen.
W How sweet of you two!
M I made bacon and eggs, orange juice, toast, and coffee.
W It looks delicious. Thanks again.

Unit 8 Making Comparisons

KEY EXPRESSIONS

1. (C) 2. (A) 3. (B) 4. (E) 5. (D)

WARM-UP

1. (A) 2. (A) 3. (B) 4. (B) 5. (A)

LISTEN FOR IT

1. (A) 2. (A) 3. (B) 4. (A) 5. (A)

TRUE OR FALSE

1. (A) F (B) F
2. (A) T (B) F
3. (A) F (B) F

LISTENING PRACTICE

1. (C) 2. (A) 3. (A) 4. (D) 5. (B)
6. (C)

DICTATION 1

A.

1. It rains more in Seattle than in London.
2. Becky sings much better than Jill.
3. On the test, Ron got a C, but Joe got an A.
4. The blue car isn't as expensive as the white one.
5. Mr. Lee works 10 hours more per week than Mr. Kim does.

B.

I have three wonderful children. The oldest, Beth, will be in college next year. Next is Danny, who is 15, and then 12-year-old Peter. Danny is the most athletic. Peter likes some sports, but Beth doesn't play any sports at all. She loves music and can sing well and play several musical instruments. Peter seems interested in music, but we'll see. Danny isn't musical at all. All three are smart, and I wouldn't dare say which one I think is the smartest.

C.

I like school a lot. My favorite subject is science. I find it the most interesting, but also the most difficult. I usually get Bs in that class. The easiest class by far is English. P.E. is the most fun—I love playing sports. I find math class pretty boring, but not nearly as boring as history. That's the worst.

LISTENING TEST

1. (A) 2. (C) 3. (B) 4. (C) 5. (C)
6. (D)

DICTATION 2

A.

M Which hotel will you be staying at in Hong Kong?
W I don't know yet.
M The St. George is the most convenient, but of course is the most expensive.
W How about the Park Lane?
M It's cheap, yes, but not as cheap as the Crown Royal if you want to save money.
W Yes, but the Crown Royal is so inconvenient. It's the farthest from all the places that I want to visit.

B.

W May I help you?
M Yes, how can I get from Vienna to Budapest?
W Well, you have four choices—train, bus, boat, or air.
M Which is the cheapest?
W Bus. There are tickets from $12. The second cheapest is the train. That costs $58.
M How about the boat?
W The boat is nice, but it takes the longest time.
M How much is it?
W It's $100 one way. The flight is $190.

C.

W Have you found an apartment yet?
M No, I'm looking, but I can't decide.
W How many have you seen?
M Three. The first one was the most modern and the biggest.
W So?
M It's also the most expensive. The second one is cheaper, but the least modern.
W And the third?
M It's the cheapest, but also the smallest.
W Hmm. They all have good and bad points.

Unit 9 In the Neighborhood

KEY EXPRESSIONS

1. (B) 2. (E) 3. (C) 4. (A) 5. (D)

WARM-UP

1. (A) 2. (B) 3. (B) 4. (B) 5. (A)

LISTEN FOR IT

1. (B) 2. (A) 3. (A) 4. (A) 5. (B)

TRUE OR FALSE

1. (A) F (B) T
2. (A) T (B) T
3. (A) F (B) T

LISTENING PRACTICE

1. (B) 2. (B) 3. (C) 4. (D) 5. (C)
6. (A)

DICTATION 1

A.

1. My neighbor is so noisy at night. I can't sleep well.
2. My neighbors invite me to a barbecue at their house every summer.

3. A family of four moved into the apartment next to mine yesterday.
4. I live next door to my aunt, so I get to see my cousins almost every day.
5. I live next to a fire station, so it can be very loud at times.

B.

W Do you and your wife ever get together with your neighbors?
M We see each other socially about once a month. They often have us over for dinner.
W That' s nice. Do their children get along with your daughter?
M Oh, yes. They have a daughter who's the same age as our Becky. They are in the same class at school.

C.

W How do you like your new apartment, Steve?
M It's fine. I've finally met some of my neighbors.
W What are they like?
M The neighbors down the hall are quiet and friendly. The family upstairs are nice too, but noisy. It's a couple with two small children. One child likes to run and play a lot. The other is always jumping rope. Sometimes they start at 6:00 a.m.
W Well, that's natural. They're just kids.

LISTENING TEST

1. (C) 2. (A) 3. (A) 4. (D) 5. (C) 6. (A)

DICTATION 2

A.

M Have your new neighbors moved in yet?
W Yes. They're nice but there's already a problem.
M Are they noisy?
W It's a big family. They have four children, but they're surprisingly quiet. The problem is their dog.
M Oh, does it keep you awake at night?
W No, but it gets me up too early with its barking.
M Hmm, you might have to get used to getting up early.

B.

W What do you like about living in the suburbs, Dave?
M There are so many good things. My kids can play on the lawn in the front yard while I sit on the porch and relax. I see my neighbors all the time, and everyone waves or stops to chat when I'm sitting outside.
W Is there anything negative about the suburbs?
M Not for me. I work at the local fire station, and it's only a ten-minute walk from my house.
W Lucky you. I have to drive for an hour to get to work at the hospital.
M Yeah, I think I'm pretty lucky, and my kids live near their school, so it's good for all of us.

C.

M I hear you're having a party, Lisa.
W Yes, it's my brother's birthday, and I want to have some people over for a small celebration.
M Will it be family only?
W No, we're really good friends with our neighbors so they'll be coming too. It's going to be potluck, so everyone will bring some food or drink to share.
M That's a good idea. It will make things much easier for you.
W Yes, and some of my neighbors are really good cooks. Hey, why don't you come? My brother really likes you.
M I'd love to. What should I bring?
W How about some kind of dessert?

Unit 10 The Weather Forecast

KEY EXPRESSIONS

1. (B) 2. (D) 3. (A) 4. (E) 5. (C)

WARM-UP

1. (A) 2. (B) 3. (B) 4. (A) 5. (B)

LISTEN FOR IT

1. (B) 2. (A) 3. (B) 4. (A) 5. (B)

TRUE OR FALSE

1. (A) T (B) F
2. (A) T (B) F
3. (A) F (B) F

LISTENING PRACTICE

1. (A) 2. (C) 3. (B) 4. (C) 5. (D) 6. (A)

DICTATION 1

A.

1. Did you see the hail yesterday? It was as big as a baseball!
2. I had to take an umbrella. It was only drizzling, but I would have gotten very wet.
3. I visited Boston yesterday, but it was much colder than I had expected.
4. The thunder was so loud yesterday. My cat hid under my bed!
5. It was so hot yesterday—much hotter than it usually is in May.

B.

W I'm fed up with this weather.
M Why? I thought you liked the rain.
W Not this much! And I'm off work next week. Is it supposed to rain a lot next week?
M No, it's going to be fairly dry.
W Good. Maybe I'll be able to go hiking during my week off. I really don't want to spend my holiday sitting at home watching TV.
M You know, it is possible to go hiking in the rain.
W Yeah, I guess so. But it's more fun when it's sunny.

C.

M Is it always this hot? I'm dying of heat.
W No, we're having a heat wave. It's usually around 35°C, but this week it's 40°.
M I don't know how you can live here! I'm glad I'm only visiting.
W You get used to the heat when you live here. I mean, when I visit you in Canada in the summer, I feel kind of cold. When you are wearing shorts and a T-shirt, I always need a sweater.
M Oh, that's true. You always ask me to turn off the air conditioning when you visit me.

LISTENING TEST

1. (B) 2. (C) 3. (B) 4. (D) 5. (B)
6. (A)

DICTATION 2

A.

W The sky is getting darker and darker.
M Yes, and it's getting cold. I think a storm is coming.
W Is it supposed to rain a lot today?
M Yes, and there may be some thunder and lightning.
W We'd better get inside before it starts pouring rain.
M Good idea. And you know how scared I am of lightning.
W Yes, I remember that time we were on the golf course during a storm. You looked so scared! But the sky was so beautiful.

B.

M What's the weather forecast for this weekend?
W The weather lady said it should be warmer, but there's a chance of rain.
M Do you know what the temperature might be?
W She said we can expect lows in the mid-50s and highs in the low 60s.
M That doesn't sound too bad. It's much better than the hail we had yesterday.

C.

W I'm thinking of visiting New York. You've been there, haven't you, Tom?
M Yes, I went there last spring.
W How was the weather in New York last spring? Is that a good time to go?
M It was sunny, but the mornings and nights were a little cold. The afternoons were nice. I was there in March, but I think April would be better. Spring is definitely better than winter for a trip. The city can get a lot of snow in winter, and the summers get really hot.
W OK, I'll book a flight for April. I've always wanted to go there.

Unit 11 My Day

KEY EXPRESSIONS

1. (B) 2. (C) 3. (E) 4. (A) 5. (D)

WARM-UP

1. (A) 2. (B) 3. (B) 4. (B) 5. (A)

LISTEN FOR IT

1. (B) 2. (A) 3. (A) 4. (B) 5. (B)

TRUE OR FALSE

1. (A) F (B) F
2. (A) F (B) T

3. (A) T (B) T

LISTENING PRACTICE

1. (B) 2. (D) 3. (A) 4. (C) 5. (B)
6. (C)

DICTATION 1

A.

1. I forgot to charge my cell phone last night. I couldn't reply to my girlfriend's texts, and now she is mad at me.
2. I vacuumed the whole house before work. But while I was out, my dog made a big mess.
3. I cut myself shaving, so I had to go to work with a band aid on my face.
4. I worked out at the gym this morning. I also took a fitness class from a new trainer. Now I'm so tired.
5. I wanted to wear my green shirt, so I washed it this morning. But my dryer stopped working, and I couldn't wear the shirt after all.

B.

W Are you in the bathroom, dear?
M Yes, I am. I'm shaving. And then I need to brush my hair.
W Will you be much longer? I still need to put on my makeup.
M I'm almost done. Just give me a minute.
W OK, but please hurry. I don't want to be late.
M I know. Why don't you make the bed while you're waiting.

C.

W Did you take out the trash, Mark?
M Sorry, Mom. I completely forgot about that. Can I do it tomorrow?
W No, you know that you are supposed to do it every day.
M But Mom, it's raining.
W Well, it wasn't raining earlier. You should have taken it out before it started to rain.
M This is so unfair.

LISTENING TEST

1. (D) 2. (C) 3. (A) 4. (B) 5. (D)
6. (D)

DICTATION 2

A.

M Do you do any exercise, Briana?
W Yes, I work out every other day: usually weight lifting. And I walk to school every day.
M Do you still play tennis?
W Not anymore, but I took up golf last year. I'm getting quite good. What about you, Chris? Are you into any sports?
M Not really. But I ride my bike a lot. I used to take the subway to work, but it took about 45 minutes. If I ride my bike, I can get to the restaurant in 30 minutes.
W That's convenient.

B.

W What do you do every evening?
M I come home from school at 4:30. I usually do my homework until 6:30 and then I have dinner.
W Do you ever help your mother cook dinner?
M Yes, sometimes. But I can't make tasty food like my mom does. I always wash the dishes after dinner.
W That's nice of you. Who does the laundry in your household?
M My mom. She says I don't get the clothes clean enough.
W Same here. My mom washes all of my clothes.

C.

M Can I borrow your phone, Jenny?
W Sure. Did you forget to charge yours again, Tom?
M Yeah. And I have to call my dad to let him know I'm about to leave.
W Do you call him every day?
M Yeah, he likes to know where I am.
W I seldom call my mom and dad. But I do send texts.
M I think most people send texts, but my dad always wants me to call him. He says texts are for lazy people.
W And I guess he likes to hear your voice.
M Maybe.

Unit 12 Let's Talk

KEY EXPRESSIONS

1. (D) 2. (E) 3. (A) 4. (C) 5. (B)

WARM-UP

1. (B) 2. (A) 3. (A) 4. (B) 5. (B)

LISTEN FOR IT

1. (A) 2. (B) 3. (A) 4. (A) 5. (A)

TRUE OR FALSE

1. (A) T (B) T
2. (A) F (B) T
3. (A) T (B) F

LISTENING PRACTICE

1. (B) 2. (C) 3. (B) 4. (D) 5. (D)
6. (A)

DICTATION 1

A.

1. Hi, this is Brian Tanaka. I got your message, and I'm returning your call.
2. Can I speak to Anita Walker at extension 302?
3. Hi, Mary. It looks like you can't come to the phone. I just wanted to let you know that I won't be home for dinner.
4. I'm calling about your advertisement on your website. Do you still have any of the pink cakes left?
5. Hey, Amanda! Did you get my text? Call me back! I need to talk to you.

B.

W Directory Assistance.
M May I have the number for Tom Leeds in Denver, Colorado?
W Thank you. I'd like to check the name. Is the last name R-E-E-D?
M No, it's L-E-E-D-S.
W I see. Just a moment. The number is 515-739-0882. May I help you with anything else?
M No. That's all, thank you.
W Have a great day.

C.

M Hey, Lisa. I want to call my old homestay family in Japan. How do I make an international call? I've never done it before.
W That's easy. Well, first you'll need to enter the country code.
M OK, let me just look that up… Got it. It's 82… No, it's 81 for Japan.
W So just dial the country code, then the area code. Then just call the phone number.
M That sounds easy.
W It is! Just let me know if you have any trouble getting through.

LISTENING TEST

1. (C) 2. (C) 3. (A) 4. (B) 5. (D)
6. (B)

DICTATION 2

A.

M Hello?
W1 Hello. Is that Kevin? This is Helen Green. Can I speak to your mother?
M Yes. Let me pass the phone to her… Mom! It's for you!
W2 Hello?
W1 Hi, Lisa. It's Helen. Are you free tomorrow? I have the day off work and I thought it might be nice to meet for lunch.
W2 Definitely. Do you want to go to that new place on Broadway?
W1 You read my mind! Why don't I pick you up at 11:30?
W2 I'll be ready!

B.

W I'm trying to make a call, but I can't get a good signal.
M Really? I'm not having any trouble. You have the same kind of phone as me.
W The problem is not the phone. It's the network. I get really bad service. I even have to pay extra for caller ID. I hate it. What phone company do you use?
M Mobile Com. They have the best coverage.
W Hmm, I've seen their advertisements. They have that really annoying man promoting the service.
M He might be annoying, but the service is good. You should switch.

C.

M How's your new job going, You Jung?

W It's great. I love it. I telecommute three days a week, so it's very convenient.

M Isn't it difficult to have meetings? I mean, you don't spend much time in the office.

W Oh, that's not a problem at all. We use various computer programs, and we do a lot of video conferences.

M Of course. But don't you find it difficult to concentrate when you are not in the same room as your co-workers?

W Not really. And the meetings are usually much shorter than when we meet at the office.

Intensive Listening Training is a three-book series designed to develop the aural comprehension skills of English language learners. Each unit focuses on real-life themes and introduces typical English speech routines. Listening tasks in each unit range from testing discrete listening items, to checking general comprehension of short dialogs and talks, to completing dictation pages. Each level in the *Intensive Listening Training* series includes more than 180 minutes of audio input for learners to use for practice as they hone their English aural skills.

Features

- Thematically organized vocabulary including common spoken collocations
- Listening tasks developed around individual sentences, short dialogs, and short talks
- Graded practice materials to support listening skill development for high-beginning to intermediate learners
- Conversational dialogs and short talks written in natural English
- Dictation activities to reinforce listening skills
- Full transcripts and answer keys included in student book

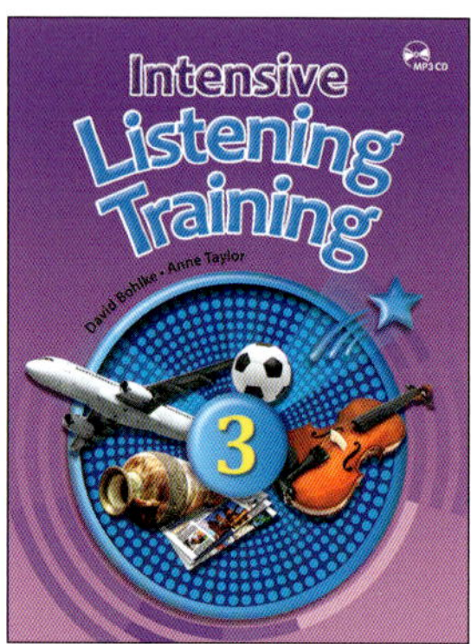

Seed Learning

www.seed-learning.com/ILT